AMERICA RESTORED

CAROL M. HIGHSMITH AND TED LANDPHAIR

PHOTOGRAPHS BY CAROL M. HIGHSMITH

THE PRESERVATION PRESS

NATIONAL TRUST FOR HISTORIC PRESERVATION

The Preservation Press
National Trust for Historic Preservation
1785 Massachusetts Avenue, N.W.
Washington, D.C. 20036

The National Trust for Historic Preservation is the only private, nonprofit organization chartered by Congress to encourage public participation in the preservation of sites, buildings, and objects significant in American history and culture. In carrying out this mission, the National Trust fosters an appreciation of the diverse character and meaning of our American cultural heritage and preserves and revitalizes the livability of our communities by leading the nation in saving America's historic environments.

Support for the National Trust is provided by membership dues, contributions, and a matching grant from the National Park Service, U.S. Department of the Interior, under provisions of the National Historic Preservation Act of 1966. The opinions expressed here do not necessarily reflect the views or policies of the Interior Department.

Printed in Singapore by Tien Wah Press
5 4 3 2 1   98 97 96 95 94

Library of Congress Cataloging in Publication Data

Highsmith, Carol M., 1946–

America restored / Carol M. Highsmith and Ted Landphair; photographs by Carol M. Highsmith.
    p.   cm.
Includes bibliographical references.
ISBN 0–89133–228–6
1. Historic buildings — United States. 2. Historic buildings — United States — Conservation and restoration. 3. Historic buildings — United States — Pictorial works. 4. Architecture — United States. 5. Architecture — United States — Conservation and restoration.
6. Architecture — United States — Pictorial works. I. Landphair, Ted, 1942– . II. Title.
E159.H65 1994   93–32365
973–dc20   CIP

Designed by Robert Wiser and Lisa Markowitz of Meadows & Wiser, Washington, D.C.

Cover: The huge Jamesway barn, part of the Wells Reserve at Laudholm Farm, Wells, Maine (see p. 148). The reserve offers seven miles of nature trails through a salt marsh, a forest, and fields.

PHOTOGRAPHY FOR *AMERICA RESTORED* WAS MADE POSSIBLE IN PART

BY A MAJOR GRANT FROM THE GOODYEAR TIRE AND RUBBER COMPANY.

Transportation support was provided by the Hertz Corporation.

Contents

Acknowledgments

To express properly our gratitude to the people who helped make *America Restored* possible would take 102 lengthy notations—one for every site we photographed and profiled. Our travels to all 50 states and the District of Columbia were inspiring highlights of a hard year, as we grew to appreciate the profound contribution made to America's historic fabric by some of the talented people at local and state preservation societies, volunteer organizations, and the hospitality industry.

Site selection was greatly eased by the skillful support of the regional offices of the National Trust for Historic Preservation—in particular, the Mountain/Plains office in Denver, the Northeast office in Boston, and the Western office in San Francisco. Some of the chosen sites are administered by the National Park Service or the U.S. Forest Service, and we found the administrators and rangers of both agencies to be enthusiastic and insightful. More than once, we gave thanks as citizens for the historic and beautiful legacy that they protect and nurture. What a bleak place America would be without them. Special thanks, too, to the National Endowment for the Arts, Design Arts Program, whose grant to Carol Highsmith gave us the impetus to undertake so ambitious a project.

Nor would we have accomplished as much in so many places and in so short a time without the great talent and high spirits of our dedicated professional family. Dorothy M. Jones played the telephone like a symphony, kept us informed and in touch, and smoothed our way to many wonderful experiences in some of the most unlikely crannies of America. Dave Hofeling worked wonders in the darkroom at all hours of the day, night, and week, with the kind of commitment and skill that portend a magnificent career.

Without the comforting assurance that a trusty Hertz rental car would be ready, waiting, and able to handle our 12 oversized pieces of luggage and camera equipment at each site, we could not have made our rounds or have been in the energetic frame of mind with which we tried to approach each assignment. Hertz was there every time, every place, and ever-helpful. And the physical and logistical burden would have been far greater had not Kathy Houde of Calumet Photographic stepped in to facilitate our obtaining lightweight, travel-ready equipment.

There are two sources of pride that we take from the *America Restored* experience. One, of course, is in the final product. The other is in Rob Landphair, a special young person who kept our house, our wits, and our trust and confidence in order during our many forays. Cameras and cars, airplane reservations and appointments can be replaced or rescheduled if need be, but there's no replacing the love and support of so fine a son.

Carol M. Highsmith and Ted Landphair

Introduction

One day in 1989, coauthors Carol Highsmith and Ted Landphair were rummaging through the National Park Service's files on America's great landmarks. The wife-and-husband team had in mind a book of national scope about the many remarkable efforts to preserve and rebuild the nation's threatened historical heritage. As they browsed through folders about one great monument, battlefield, or national park after another, park service staff specialist Michael Auer remarked, "These accomplishments are wonderful, but did you realize that since 1976 *private* businesses and individuals in this country have poured $13 billion of their own money into restoration?"

No, the authors did not know. Thirteen *billion* dollars in private funds—actually $16 billion through 1992—had helped breathe new life into shopworn office buildings, decrepit country stores, abandoned mills, and creaky old mansions. And billions more had undoubtedly funded restorations the park service knew nothing about.

Highsmith and Landphair would soon see for themselves the results of the staggering donations of money and time. Did these private labors to restore the treasures of America's built environment signal some profound sea change in America's attitude toward its own antiquity? How had tepid appreciation of neat old house museums and historical parks turned into a hell-bent commitment to rescue and refurbish everything from one-room country schoolhouses to whole city neighborhoods? Was it simply avarice, striking while the generous rehabilitation tax credits were hot? Or had the dogged persistence of true believers like the National Trust for Historic Preservation and state preservation offices finally driven the preservation message into the American consciousness?

The answers came clearer as Highsmith and Landphair broadened the scope of their national landmarks project. They traveled to every state, selecting from hundreds of candidates two of the most remarkable restoration sites in each. The chosen projects, from an estuarian research farm in Maine to a former leper-colony church in Hawaii, together testify to a powerful restoration revolution. Highsmith's lens captured a visual feast: great homes and business buildings, churches and depots, theaters and hotels. Also documented were delightfully eclectic restorations: a packet steamer, carousels, street clocks, covered bridges, two former municipal water-treatment plants, a destroyer, and even a mining tipple. Landphair's conversations with the dedicated restorers gave a context to these remarkable achievements.

The authors called the resulting collection *America Restored* rather than *America Preserved,* because the book documents a determination not just to hold onto something, but to reassert its worth and beauty and craftsmanship for all to enjoy. *America Restored* is more than another nostalgic journey: There's some swagger amid these sweet success stories. Investors don't sink $16 billion into mere nostalgia.

Almost a century-and-a-half of precedent backs up this gush of good works. America's restoration fever grew out of the tenacity of a lone woman, Ann Pamela Cunningham, who in 1853 formed the "Mount Vernon Ladies" to save George Washington's Virginia home and put it in public trust. Similar efforts by others at Monticello, Old Sturbridge, and Colonial Williamsburg set early standards for the "historic experience" at house and plantation museums. The idea of displaying the historical and technological artifacts of our social history for public benefit and enjoyment was laid. Still, these attractions were few and far between. For a very long time, other historic buildings were seen as either aging eyesores—ripe for demolition—or mere warehouses in which their contents—furniture, ceramics, glass—were the allurement. Only as more and more great buildings were threatened or lost did the structures themselves take center stage.

By the mid-20th century, however, when wrecking crews toppled historic building after building in cities across the country in a misguided effort at "urban renewal," it was clear that the salvation of historic architecture could not be left to museum associations alone. Instead, says National Trust Vice President Peter H. Brink, there was a realization that preservation depended on "people in thousands of communities across the United States saving the most historic—or at least the most handsome and impressive—house in town." Even before Congress established the National Trust in 1949 to keep a watch on historic treasures, cities like New Orleans, Savannah, Vicksburg, and Charleston had set up watchdog commissions that simply would not let their historic quarters be adulterated or lost. As the National Register of Historic Places, created in 1966, quickly gained cachet, the prestige of a register listing came to be marketable. While it alone could not save a building, a National Register designation aided efforts to garner the local historic status that could.

Sometimes it was too late. Spencer Ruff, an architect who restored the old Willey & Williams office building in Sioux Falls, South Dakota [p. 270], points to a debate he witnessed about whether to save the old courthouse in tiny Slayton, Minnesota. "I remember well that one of the county commissioners said, 'We don't have any history around here,'" he says. "There were some ardent preservationists who testified, but the building got torn down, and [the county] built a rather ugly one-story building in its place."

In the larger cities, Lyndon Johnson's 1966 "Model Cities" program, which had extended a "promise of new life" or "urban renewal," turned urban neighborhoods into concrete ghettos; people who had never thought of themselves as "preservationists" snapped to. To see vibrant urban intercourse snuffed out by sterile high rises and parking lots sent preservationists to the parapets.

After enough losses to wrecking balls and bulldozers, cities in every state formed local historic districts, sacrosanct from pernicious development, and state historic preservation officers won the right to intervene to stop federal actions that would adversely affect historic resources. Preservation became an essential part of comprehensive planning. No longer did fanciful planners simply wonder what new under the sun they could devise; they began looking more closely at the jewels they already had. And governments appreciated preservation's more practical aspects— that pumping life into moribund neighborhoods, and sometimes rescuing just one beloved structure, improves public safety, increases property values, brings in tax revenues, and can make tourist attractions out of architectural discards.

The fireplace was part of
Wright's support structure.
The much-admired geometric
"grammar" of his intricate
glass-and-board walls neglected
one detail: insulation.

Opposite: There are few curves,
and even less overstuffed
comfort, in a Wright house.
Every angular form, such as
the Rosenbaums' table, seems
to have a function.

Harrison Brothers Hardware

Huntsville, Alabama

SICK. That's all the hand-printed, cardboard sign on the door said one October morning in 1983 when John Harrison did not show up for work, and Harrison Brothers Hardware store failed to open on a weekday for the first time in years. John and his late brother Daniel had worked there since they were stock boys for their father, and now only John, a pack rat who made Fibber McGee look tidy, knew exactly where each screw and strainer, trowel and ventilator clamp, washboard and radio tube could be found.

That took some doing in a store cluttered with hundreds of horseshoes, bins of nails and washers and walking canes, and 20 years' worth of Huntsville newspapers that the brothers had stuck behind the counter. In the basement were spent bullets and broken jugs and stove grates. There were secret stashes, too, that volunteers from the nonprofit Historic Huntsville Foundation found when they entered the store a few weeks later, after John's death: 1920 nudist magazines, more than a few bourbon bottles, and a book on how to join the Ku Klux Klan.

The foundation, which tries to find buyers for old homes but had never owned anything, had bought the store from the brothers' 18 heirs to keep it from being gutted and turned into office space. Soon volunteers were wading into the dust and grime and mold, their noses and mouths sheathed in masks beneath brown bags used to protect their heads. The store's exterior was faithfully repainted in the original forest green shade, and cracked windows were replaced.

The hardware sits on the downtown square, across from the courthouse where, long before the Redstone Arsenal had turned Huntsville into "Rocket City" in the 1950s, wagons heaped with tobacco and cotton and peaches jammed the streets. Instead of turning the old store into a museum, foundation members resolved to try to keep it running, with one accommodation: They'd turn one-half of the store, where the Harrisons had sold crockery and Tennessee rocking chairs, into a gift shop, while keeping the hardware side open for business. There was plenty for customers to gape at: the old painted safe, the rope-pulled freight lift, and the chest-high "standing desk" where yellowed invoices dating to 1885 were stacked. Or the hand-cranked cash register, whose bottom drawer was stuffed with fuses, tire stems, a wire brush, a handful of buckeyes, a bill from Huntsville's Hotel Twickenham, a guarantee from the Harrisons' 1939 Ford panel truck, and a shoelace tied to a tag that read "For John's Shoe." In another drawer, store manager Aggie Carter found a remedy for colic that included "25 drops, chloroform."

Carter and about 100 people who volunteer at Harrison's can be talked into parting with an old curiosity so long as it's not the last one left in the store. Ultimately, Carter says, the foundation would like to get out of the retail business, turn the Harrison place over to someone who will treasure and preserve it, and move on to saving another piece of Old Huntsville.

Presiding over the clutter, the old hand-cranked cash register was a hodgepodge as bizarre as John and Daniel Harrison's inventory system. But the brothers knew where to find every item in the store.

Riverboat Nenana

Fairbanks, Alaska

At Alaskaland, Fairbanks's 44-acre heritage park full of pioneer artifacts, you come upon the *Nenana,* a remarkably restored remnant of Alaska's nautical history. A sternwheel packet steamer that once plied the interior rivers of the Last Frontier, *Nenana* is the second-largest wooden vessel in the world (next to San Francisco's sidewheeler ferry *Eureka*). It carried 200 tons of cargo, 16 passengers, and a crew of 35. There were no "wedding cake" decks, no gay calliope, although the boat did offer cozy mahogany-fitted staterooms and fine dining.

Nenana *pushes a barge loaded with heavy equipment on the Yukon River in 1949. She also carried passengers. (Anchorage Museum of History and Art)*

The *Nenana* was operated in the 1930s and 1940s by the Alaska Railroad, the only rail line owned by the federal government. The riverboat spent snowy, dark Alaska winters on grids high off the riverbank in the town of Nenana, away from damaging ice floes. Each May the skids would be greased with tallow, the boiler refired, and the *Nenana* would be off again.

Reconditioned in 1952–53, the boat was leased by a barge company that failed to turn a profit, so the government sold it for $40,000 to a Fairbanks Chamber of Commerce offshoot. *Nenana* functioned briefly as a museum and floating hotel, then sat idle, wantonly looted by vandals. In 1965 the riverboat was floated to Alaskaland, where it was crudely renovated for the 1967 Alaska Centennial. The addition of a "Sand Bar" restaurant, a bar, and a kitchen did great violence to the historic fabric of the boat, and dry rot from moisture trapped between the frigid outside surfaces and the toasty-warm interior set in throughout the boat's hold and decks.

The boat was moved to a cradle out of the water, where, in 1987, a remarkable restoration effort began. It started when Jack Williams, a surveyor and owner of an Alaskaland restaurant, assembled the Fairbanks Historical Preservation Foundation. The nonprofit group was confronted with a $2 million restoration estimate. "We decided to do it right," Williams says. Money came from a city bed tax, grants from the state, county and National Trust for Historic Preservation, and from local "pull-tab" wagering. "The daunting task was the hand-scraping, sanding, and filling of every square inch, inside and out," Williams says.

In 1989 children from Fairbanks's University Park School presented Jack Williams with a check for $1,000, raised from selling brownies and T-shirts and from shoveling snow. One girl stepped forward and said, "Mr. Williams, we got this money so you can help fix *our* boat. And don't you worry. We'll take good care of it when we grow up."

Before finding a dry dock, the Nenana was moored in a manmade pond, rotting and almost splitting apart from structural fatigue. Adding a restaurant and bar further desecrated her inside.

Opposite: Volunteer sign painter Vern Hines adds the final touch to the Nenana restoration. Restorers had to remove 22 layers of paint before repainting.

Top: The Nenana's steering wheel looks out over a decidedly earthly view of Alaskaland's natural setting.

Above: The rich, mahogany-paneled "saloon deck" had no saloon, but it sat up to 40 for dinner.

Overleaf: The winch system included spars called "walking legs" that could swing out and literally walk the boat off a sandbar, should Nenana get stuck at low tide.

Russian Bishop's House

Sitka, Alaska

There was once a Colonial Alaska whose flag was Imperial Russian. Agents of the Russian-American Company first settled, trapped, and fished there in the 18th century, accompanied by Russian Orthodox missionaries who ministered among the native Aleuts and Eskimos from what would become the bustling colonial capital of New Archangel—now the tranquil fishing and tourist town of Sitka. "God is in His heaven," the missioners said, "and the Tsar is far away."

From 1841 to 1843, ethnic Finnish shipwrights in this "Paris of the Pacific" built a grand spruce-and-log house—painted the company's standard golden yellow with a red roof—for Ivan Veniaminov, Bishop Innocent. To keep out the cold and perpetual dampness, this "ecclesiastical palace" incorporated energy-saving features like sand insulation between floor and ceiling planks. Not wallpaper, but glued Cyrillic manuscripts, ledgers, and even meal menus, sealed cracks in the walls. The bishop's and staff beds, still displayed, were inordinately short, as it was the health practice to sleep in a near-sitting position, propped against pillows.

Weakened by territorial losses to Turkey and Britain in the Crimean War of 1853–56 and having decimated the population of furred animals, most Russians abandoned Alaska, which became an American possession with the famous $7.2 million "Seward's Folly" purchase in 1867. But it was not until 1969 that the leaking, rotting bishop's house was abandoned by the church. Three years later its new owner, the National Park Service, began a $5 million, 16-year restoration. The structure was dismantled—every board numbered—and rebuilt to its 1853 appearance. Wall coverings, notably a menu for a Shrovetide week that included fish soup, pea soup, "fish hamburgers," pancakes, and Russian *pirogi* pies, were repaired and remounted. The restored bishop's chapel was reconsecrated and reopened for services. So vivid were its heavenly blue walls and refurbished icons that Innocent himself would have felt right at home.

Opposite: Bishop Innocent's effects included numerous crosses and religious medallions. Furniture was shipped to New Archangel from Siberia or the Russian settlement in what is now California.

The residence of the "Bishop of Kamchatka, the Kuriles, and the Aleutian Islands" also housed the Chapel of the Annunciation and a school for Russian and mixed-blood children.

University of Arizona's Old Main

Tucson, Arizona

How grand the first building at Arizona Territory's pioneer college looked on October 1, 1891, as the students and their professors, breaking from the first day of classes, no doubt sought a snatch of breeze on the veranda. "European adaptation," the University Building's architect, James W. Creighton of Phoenix, called the British-style structure, with its ventilated mansard roof, wide outdoor staircases, and lower level sunk into the loose desert soil to keep a grip on every wisp of nighttime chill. Above the second story rose four ornamental towers, signifying, as Creighton would later say, "the heights to which education might rise."

These were the hallowed halls, not of ivy, but of cacti and greasewood, for the building lay four miles from Tucson in the middle of a Sonoran Desert mesa. The whole "Arizona School of Agriculture" was six faculty members and six students. University Building also housed 26 preparatory pupils, taught by the same teachers. Male students lived there, as did married professors and their families. Some among them wrapped in damp sheets and slept on the veranda on torrid summer nights. At first the building housed classrooms and agriculture laboratories, a mess hall, and even the territorial weather bureau. By 1919 it was already deemed antiquated; a master plan that year shows it expunged. In 1940 the university president asked that Old Main—a name it acquired in 1928—be torn down, and down it might have come had not the Department of the Navy used the space for its World War II "indoctrination school." The navy spent $89,000 stabilizing, and thus saving, Old Main.

After the war it often sat empty or housed a potpourri of programs too small to have a building of their own. During the 1960s, the university's own student newspaper labeled Old Main a "monstrosity." But in 1972, a small group of preservationists managed to get it listed in the National Register of Historic Places, giving the University of Arizona a landmark whether it wanted it or not. In 1987 the university began restoring the old building. Work crews repointed the exterior brick and returned the basement to a turn-of-the-century look, reexposing patterned-metal ceilings and adding period light fixtures. They uncovered, and saved, original brick arches behind a hallway wall. Outside, out went generic flowers and shrubs, and back came a virtual Southwest arboretum, from sour oranges to the obligatory saguaro cacti.

At its rededication on March 8, 1988, a speaker redubbed the university's onetime "monstrosity" the "core of this campus, the center of campus, the spirit of campus, the beacon of campus." Robert Wrenn, the university's director of student services, says, "Today we have programs here in the building to help prepare students who are not quite ready for the university. A century ago, the six faculty members were doing the same thing with all but six of their students. In a way, history has repeated itself."

For many years, Old Main was the University of Arizona. Faculty and students lived, as well as taught and studied, inside its walls, four sweltering desert miles from town.

Almer Store

Helena, Arkansas

Many a splendid, historic American structure has been saved just in the nick of time, as it was about to be bought or bulldozed. But the Almer Store, in the drowsy Mississippi River Delta town of Helena, was rescued *past* the nick of time, while it was actually *being* torn down.

The simple little structure had been built in 1872 by a Swiss immigrant, Ulrick Amacher (later changed to Almer), who, with his wife, had floated from his previous home in Missouri down to Helena on a flatboat, on which he had built a crude house. They kept cows in the nearby Arkansas hills, herded them down to the dock for milking, and made butter and cheese that they sold to make a living. Then they relocated to a town lot large enough to keep their cows.

There, Ulrick Almer constructed a primitive, yet imaginatively ornamented, combination home and dairy store. Horizontal, hard-planed cypress planks laid between vertical grooved posts made up the walls, and waxed strings shoved into the cracks kept out the wind. The gabled roof was covered with machine-cut cypress shingles, probably crafted on the premises by Almer himself. Customers entered through a large double front door, and light came through tall windows covered by folding shutters. These pragmatic features contrasted with the delicate gingerbread border underneath the eaves.

Eventually the Almers built a separate house out back. The store remained in the family for nearly 70 more years and was occupied by various tenants, including a grocer. Finally it sat empty, looking like a weather-beaten Ozark shack. So badly did the roof leak that the flooring rotted and gave way, and any vestiges of paint that had not long ago blistered disappeared.

In 1974 the property's heir sold what remained of the store to a Helena plumber, whose men were cheerfully demolishing the structure when the plumber got an agitated phone call. Annetta Beauchamp, one of the organizers of the Phillips County Foundation for Historic Preservation, implored him to desist so the foundation could seek funds to save the structure. The plumber agreed, and the money soon arrived in the form of an Arkansas American Revolution Bicentennial grant, matched by local donations. The foundation quickly drafted plans for an authentic restoration of the Almer store in time for the 1976 national bicentennial. Dozens of townspeople showed up to clean, paint, and stock the store. Says Beauchamp, "It was kind of like Jimmy Stewart in *It's a Wonderful Life*." A second restoration occurred in the 1980s, when an old lean-to was re-created using materials obtained from a house that was being razed. Both efforts were as faithful to the original as the foundation's limited budget would allow.

Almer Store is now the last stop on Annetta Beauchamp's historic tour of Helena. It's the one place visitors can spend some money, not only helping local craftspeople make a dollar, but also keeping the humble cheesemaker's store around a while longer.

The Almers lived for a time to the right of their dairy store in what was little more than a lean-to, part of which was fashioned of boards from their flatboat. The humble cheesemaker's store, constructed from floor to ceiling of hard-planed cypress planks, is now an outlet for local craftspeople — the last stop on a heritage tour of Helena.

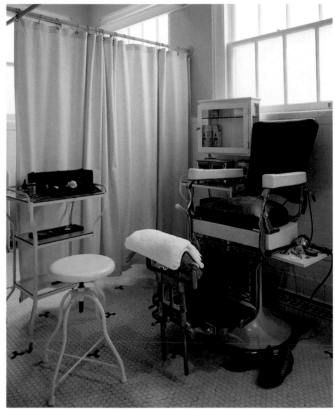

Opposite: In the men's bath court, an Indian maid pours waters for explorer Hernando De Soto. Light streams through an 8,000-piece glass ceiling depicting mermaids, Neptune's daughter, and a male admirer.

Like the ladies' parlor and music room across the way, the gentlemen's billiard room opened onto a balcony where bathers could sunbathe in the nude.

The Fordyce included a dozen or more specialized treatment facilities, such as this "Chiropodist Room." Others were the napping rooms, a massage parlor, and a complete "Department of Mechano-Therapy."

Waterworks Building

Beverly Hills, California

Shrouded behind concrete courtyard walls and overgrown eucalyptus trees, the Spanish mission-style building with the red-tile roof and Sevillian minaret looked for all the world like a convent. Inside, with its labyrinthine pipes and diodes, deep settling tanks of water, and vats of chemicals, it had the sinister look of a Lon Chaney movie set. While it lasted, engineer Arthur Taylor's 1927 Waterworks Building filtered the well water of Beverly Hills's *beau monde* and, by keeping the local water supply self-sustaining, helped stave off annexation by gargantuan Los Angeles. No wonder the waterworks was fondly known as the "Beverly Hills Independence Hall."

In 1976 the city council at last hooked into the Metropolitan Water District, the spigots were turned off at the old waterworks, and for more than a decade it stood empty. In 1988, the city decided to rid itself of the building. Before the wreckers could arrive, a group of neighbors and preservationists, calling themselves "Friends of the Waterworks," filed suit to stop demolition and force the city to complete a study of other possible uses for the structure.

At precisely this time, the Academy of Motion Picture Arts and Sciences was looking for a new home for its library and archives. The academy asked Los Angeles restoration architect Frances Offenhauser to give the old waterworks a look. Offenhauser was one of those passersby who assumed it was a "defunct monastery." Carrying flashlights like a search party from a Spielberg movie, she and academy officials felt their way through the spooky space. They found it free of columns, offering interesting light, and so "muscular" (Offenhauser's word) that it could easily support the library's 18,000 books and 12,000 films. The academy signed a 55-year lease, and a $6 million restoration began. Contractors cleared tons of pipe and damaged concrete from aeration tanks and lime pits, at one point stacking the rubble in a pile higher than the building. The main ceiling was enhanced to produce the sweeping, coffered arches of the new Cecil B. DeMille Reading Room. Outside, settling tanks gave way to a sympathetic new 10,000-square-foot wing, housing the archive's five million still photographs.

The metamorphosis delights the 20,000 researchers who visit the building each year, as it no doubt would have pleased the Beverly Hills citizen who pushed hardest for the original Waterworks Building in 1927. He was the academy's first president, Douglas Fairbanks.

Few in Beverly Hills knew that this "convent" was a water-treatment plant, or that the minaret was a disguised smokestack, quietly disgorging hydrogen sulfide sediment.

Sheraton Palace Hotel

San Francisco, California

The Palace. Its very name stood for the swaggering New West. World's largest hotel. Gutted by fire in the Great San Francisco Earthquake of 1906, and then reconstructed. Host to presidents and royalty like Warren G. Harding and King David Kalakaua of Hawaii, who both died in the hotel. Sold to the Sheraton Corporation and later to Kyo-ya Limited. Closed for renovation, during which the 6.9-scale Loma Prieta quake of 1989 struck the city. Saved by preservationists, and finally reopened in 1991 after a $150 million restoration.

The $5 million Palace Hotel was built in 1875 by San Francisco pioneers William Sharon and William Chapman Ralston. To make their hotel earthquake-resistant, the owners ordered steel reinforcing, plus four artesian wells and a 630,000-gallon reservoir. As a result the Palace almost survived the Great Quake—until firefighters pumped its water reserves dry, and fire gutted the building.

There was no question that the hotel, renowned for its "Palace Gold" dinner service and epic banquets, would be rebuilt. In 1909 New York architects Breck Parkham Trowbridge and Goodhue Livingston added two stories and turned the Grand Court off the carriage entrance into one of San Francisco's most elegant dining rooms. For almost a half century, the Palace dazzled. In 1954 Mrs. William B. Johnston, granddaughter of cofounder Sharon, sold the hotel to the Sheraton Corporation, which began a modernization program. But the Palace, like many grand downtown hotels, lost its cachet and desired clientele.

In 1973 the Honolulu-based and Japanese-owned Kyo-ya company purchased the Sheraton Palace, leaving management to ITT-Sheraton. By the 1980s it was clear the hotel, with its antiquated steam radiators and lack of air conditioning, would have to shut down or undergo substantial renovation. Kyo-ya chose the latter. As renovation progressed, the October 17, 1989, earthquake struck. Luckily the hotel was closed at the time; fortunately, too, nearly 100 chandeliers and the Garden Court's 70,000-piece stained-glass ornamental dome had just been removed for restoration. When the gloriously reappointed Palace reopened on April 3, 1991, Nancy Johnston McNear, great-great granddaughter of the Palace's first co-owner, was the first of a steady stream of appreciative San Franciscans to check in.

Two stories higher than the original, and twice as expensive at $10 million, the Palace reopened in 1909 to a banquet for 1,500. (San Francisco Public Library)

Opposite: Tacky aluminum-storefront entrance doors—a product of an ill-advised 1950s renovation—were torn away in the restoration, revealing again exquisite cast-iron doors and a marble foyer.

Overleaf: Originally a carriage courtyard, later despoiled as a nondescript exhibition space hidden behind heavy doors, the opulent Garden Court is again one of the world's most beautiful dining rooms.

Cleveholm Castle

Redstone, Colorado

Cleveholm's tale is the story of Cleve Osgood, a benevolent industrialist who not so much tamed as refined the Colorado wilderness. By 1892 Osgood, a cousin of President Grover Cleveland, had grabbed $40 million in coal claims and controlled the West's only steel mill, in Pueblo, Colorado. Osgood moved to New York, bought an entire city block and built a house on it, began annual pilgrimages to Europe, and traded stocks with fellow nouveau-aristocrats. Osgood coveted a summer address as big as the West, so in 1899 he bought 19,000 acres of the wild Crystal River Valley and—for more than $2.5 million—built Redstone, an American feudal kingdom with 84 frame cottages, a bachelors' inn, a schoolhouse, and a recreation center.

Towering over Redstone was his summer castle, Cleveholm. Cleve and his second wife, Alma, filled what writer Martie Sterling called "a transmogrified Hudson River manor with overtones of King Ludwig" with trophy heads, Tiffany lamps, ruby velvet drapes, and leather wall coverings.

Osgood lost control of his steel company, and by 1909 Redstone's 200 coke ovens were cold and the village deserted. In 1923 the "Lion of Redstone," then 72, returned with his third wife, Lucille, barely 20, a former chorus girl. Osgood died three years later, and Lucille inherited the estate, including $4.5 million in cash; she eventually sold the property in pieces.

Cleveholm became a dude ranch and later a resort inn, and in 1974 Pitkin County prevented it from being razed to make room for skiing condos. It was later rescued by Grand Junction newspaper publisher Ken Johnson, who paid $225,000 for the castle and 80 acres. Johnson and his wife, Rhodie, restored a room at a time. In 1992, for the first time in 30 years, Cleveholm made money for its owners, this time as a pensione and a haven for retreats and weddings. Capitalist Cleve Osgood, whose ashes are scattered in the valley below, would likely have approved.

Only the high and mighty got invitations to Cleve and Alma Osgood's Cleveholm, the sandstone castle of their feudal estate, shown here in 1906. (Colorado Historical Society) Opposite: The Osgoods furnished Cleveholm with treasures from their world travels and trophies of their hunts in Redstone Valley.

Colorado Chautauqua

Boulder, Colorado

In a state renowned for resorts, the Colorado Chautauqua is an anti-resort. Since 1897 people have come here, not for instant gratification or days packed with frenzied exertion, but for peace and quiet. You can tramp into the Flatiron Range of the Rockies or get up a croquet game on the green, but the workout is mostly intellectual, and the invigoration is of the soul.

The Colorado Chautauqua is a rare survivor of a self-improvement movement that swept the country when rural America—its women, especially—reached out for enlightenment. In 1874 two Sunday School directors improved upon the old New England Lyceum idea, moving provocative speakers from stuffy town halls to a sylvan setting on New York State's Lake Chautauqua, adding a study program and inviting people to pitch a tent and stay awhile.

By the turn of the century, 150 such "grand assemblies," which had become known as chautauquas, ranged from Maine to the American West. In the chautauquas' peak year, 1924, 40 million Americans—one third of the nation's population—participated. One of the most enduring assemblies began with Texas educators and railroad officials, who sent communicants by the trainload to a shady, restful park outside Boulder. The city eagerly built the visitors an auditorium, a dining hall, and a bandstand among the tents. Chautauquans got stemwinding speeches, bracing music, classes in everything from Anglo-Saxon to physics, hikes and train excursions, and informal sisterhood.

But the Depression, the advent of movies and radio, and a flapper-age disdain of preachy morality decimated chautauqua attendance. Colorado's almost died in the 1960s when Boulder became a "hippie" haven, and the smell of marijuana over-powered the campfires' scent. But the chautauquans rallied to rebuild the program and save their cottages from salivating developers. Today, visitors find 61 rental cottages, two lodges, and a community house. The park also attracts day- trippers by the tens of thousands. Gone, though, are the classes and moralizing orations.

Since 1989 the Colorado Chautauqua Association has undertaken a $2 million restoration, in which it is replacing rotted woodwork and outdated plumbing in two cottages each year. Contractors reshingled the old auditorium, shored up its sagging turrets, and replaced decayed wood. The chautauqua, which Teddy Roosevelt once called the "most American thing about America," thrives again in Boulder.

Entertainment at the Colorado Chautauqua ranged from fiery oratorial extravaganzas and great band concerts to simple front-porch jigs. (Carnegie Branch Library for Local History, Boulder)
Opposite: Woodsy serenity, idle play in the park, and vigorous hikes into the Flatiron Range are still the backbone of the chautauqua experience for both cabin owners and day-trippers.

Huntington Tavern

Norwich, Connecticut

Huntington Tavern "speaks" to Stephen P. Mack, an uncommon restorer, who in 1987 bought it and spent $500,000 reviving the defiled colonial masterpiece. As history, it speaks of pre-Revolutionary days when Simon Huntington, a Norwichtown burgher, lodged soldiers, statesmen, and travelers in cozy rooms with shallow fireplaces and nails in the plaster walls on which to hang their clothes. In 1768 Huntington tore it down, rebuilt it using all of the bricks and beams that he could salvage, and used part of his expanded tavern as the town poorhouse. Some time in the 19th century, another owner turned it into the grandest private home on the Norwich green.

To Mack, the Huntington Tavern is also art. He sees it "not as a static thing, but as a combination of the materials that went into it, the people who built it, the spaces it creates, and what is happening every day still." Mack is best known for rescuing doomed historic houses, disassembling them after photographing each tiny piece, storing the components at his farm in Ashaway, Rhode Island, and then reassembling the structures for clients in other locales. Or, as in the case of the Huntington Tavern, he will use a board here, a sconce there, to make an old property whole. "It's like an organ transplant," he says. "Never from a living donor."

Huntington Tavern's double overhang, brownstone steps, bootscraper, and original front door and hinges caught Stephen Mack's eye. The building again dominates the Norwich green.

Stephen Mack first beheld the Huntington Tavern in 1983 while working nearby—and saw a potential masterwork beneath its oxidized, crumbling red paint. Four years later he was able to purchase it and throw a most unusual open house before he started work; about 800 people showed up. Fortunately, Mack says, earlier renovation butchery had done little to change the tavern's historic fabric. He was forced to cement over the basement dirt floor because "it smelled as though three regiments of British soldiers had been buried there." He also replaced 13 missing "Indian shutters" that slide into the window jambs on the interior. In the north bedchamber he took the walls down to their 1768 surface, leaving a mottled blue-green veneer in place.

When he finished, Mack held another open house. Almost 2,000 people came; he eventually sold the tavern at a loss. He reflects, "It's very important to me that you really, truly get the best of both worlds: a house with enough amenities that you're satisfied with, but a historic house that's going to be there for the duration, hopefully another 200 years."

*Mack took the walls in
the north bedchamber down
to their 1768 surface, leaving
a mottled veneer on the
original wood paneling.*

Roseland Cottage & Ice House

Woodstock, Connecticut

What's wrong with this picture? Henry Chandler Bowen, pillar of Woodstock, a prosperous farming town of white Federal-style homes in Connecticut's northeast "Quiet Corner." Prim Congregationalist, born and reared in Woodstock, where in 1846 he built a summer house in the Gothic Revival style associated with Christian piety. Even more comfortably ensconced in Brooklyn, New York, where he, his wife, and 10 children reaped the rewards of his success in the dry-goods trade. Self-effacing amateur horticulturist with a passion for roses.

Clue: It's in the roses. Borrowing from the showy bushes in his formal parterre boxwood gardens, Bowen painted his "Roseland" cottage a shocking pink, not just once, but 13 times in the 50 years he summered here. It displayed impressive Gothic gables, vertical board-and-batten siding, scroll-cut bargeboard trim, high chimneys and finials, generous verandas, stained-glass and quatrefoil windows, and a room with a rare built-in bathtub.

Around Independence Day each year, Bowen threw the party of all 19th-century parties. On July 3, he presented respectable Woodstock with calling cards for an afternoon of lemonade, Strauss waltzes, and a whirl at croquet. The Fourth of July brought speeches, fireworks, and stirring music at Roseland Lake. Four sitting presidents—Ulysses S. Grant, Rutherford B. Hayes, Benjamin Harrison, and William McKinley—made the scene. Grant, after rolling a strike on the bowling alley inside Bowen's barn, lighted his customary cigar. When his host, betraying his Puritan stock, informed the general that smoking and drinking were not permitted at Roseland and asked him to stamp the stogie out, Grant obliged— but took a room that night in town.

Following Henry Bowen's death, the estate stayed in the family. After an unmarried granddaughter who had lived in the house died in 1968, relatives left it empty for three years, then sold the estate to the Society for the Preservation of New England Antiquities. The group's task was to stabilize the cottage, barn, and a distinctive 1870s ice house that had held the family privy, dovecote, and potting room. Paint had peeled inside and out on all the structures, roofs leaked, walls sagged, and the porte cochere was near collapse. Bowen's beloved gardens had gone to seed.

In the 1980s SPNEA embarked on a $600,000 restoration of Roseland and transformation of the barn into a conference center. In the garden, former University of Connecticut horticulture professor Rudy Favretti laid out 21 beds of roses, perennials, and 4,500 annuals. All of the cottage's furnishings, save for two chairs, are original; they include settees, walnut bay-window seats, and a cast-iron hall tree and umbrella stand. Among the best-loved treasures is the Bowens' monogrammed Limoges china. Naturally, it is colored rose.

Opposite: A pink-with-dark-trim paint scheme came highly recommended by architectural authority Andrew Jackson Downing. Henry Bowen painted Roseland 13 different shades of pink during his 50 summers there.

Overleaf: Ulysses S. Grant rolled a strike on his first ball on Bowen's bowling alley, then created a scene by lighting up a self-congratulatory cigar.

Henry Bowen's granddaughter,
Sylvia Holt, poses in her
grandfather's pride and joy—
his impeccably sculpted
garden—in 1902. (Society
for the Preservation of New
England Antiquities)

Stained glass abounds in Roseland's parlors. The Gothic Revival style was favored for domestic architecture partly because of its association with sacred motifs and the sanctity of family life.

George Read II House

New Castle, Delaware

Picture the 1804 High Federal–style mansion of the scion of Delaware's first great statesman, looming over its neighbors on the strand in this manicured colonial capital. Adorn it with gardens and a vista of the Delaware River wharf where William Penn first set foot in the New World. Must be a prim, look-but-don't-touch sort of place, this George Read II House.

Au contraire. It's a veritable fun house, from the rathskeller to the dining room with its exaggerated painted wallpaper scenes. In the back parlor every so often, Read's son Charles's funeral is remembered, complete with coffin, mourning jewelry, and death mask.

Not that George II set a jovial precedent. Son of a modest, revered signer of the Declaration of Independence who was Delaware's first state governor, George II was a miserly, vainglorious lawyer who traded on his name to run for Congress, losing every time. But no one in Delaware's colonial seat (also briefly its state capital) could deny that George II's house—humbling nearby taverns and brothels with its gilded fanlights, balustrade with Grecian urns, great Palladian window, and elaborate gesso bas-reliefs on its parlor mantels—was a stunner.

George II foundered in business and died bankrupt in 1836. The property was divided among survivors and the contents sold at public auction to pay Read's debts. In 1920 the house was sold for $9,000 to the colorful Lairds—socialite Lydia and investment banker Philip—both Du Pont family in-laws. They commissioned a fanciful history of New Castle painted on wallpaper in the dining room and turned the basement meat room and larder into a sort of private speakeasy that would see ribald good times during Prohibition.

Philip Laird died in 1945; at her own passing in 1975, Lydia left the furnished house to the Historical Society of Delaware, which undertook a 10-year, $900,000 restoration. Underneath layers of wallpaper, artisans found that several surfaces had been painted bright hues—salmon pink, lime green, "Patent Yellow"—and copied the colors. Craftsmen working with dental tools restored delicate punch-and-gouge border designs in parlor woodwork.

The Lairds helped Delaware rediscover the town that had seen Penn's Quakers, Peter Stuyvesant and the Dutch, and the Swedes who occupied Fort Trinity downriver. The Read House, to which George II had tried so hard to call attention, was and remains New Castle's centerpiece.

Relatives of the house's second owner, William Couper, a prosperous bachelor who made a fortune in the China tea trade, pose on the front steps, c. 1890. (Historical Society of Delaware)
Opposite: The back parlor is draped in 1880s mourning decor, which was kept in place for up to a year. Funeral mementos—including the deceased's death mask—are displayed in another room.
Overleaf: The Lairds' basement taproom was the scene of many raucous theme parties on Halloween and other occasions. A seaplane that landed out front brought in refreshments during the Depression.

*Opposite: A portrait of
Bessie Bringhurst Galt Smith,
dressed in a Queen of Lorraine
costume that she had worn
to a party on Malta, dominates
the breakfast room.*

*Above: George Kennedy Galt
Smith and Edward Bringhurst
III launch sailing vessels in
Joseph Shipley's favorite room,
the conservatory, c. 1892.
(Rockwood Museum)
Overleaf: Only one swatch of
gray wallpaper remains in the
"Gray Bedroom"—Bessie
Bringhurst Galt Smith's room
until 1897.*

Union Station

Washington, D.C.

Master architect Daniel P. Burnham found the inspiration for his temple of transportation while visiting the Piazza della Repubblica in Rome. (Union Station Redevelopment Corporation.)
Opposite: Louis Saint-Gaudens's six 25-ton figures representing fire, electricity, agriculture, mechanics, freedom, and imagination peer down on the Union Station plaza.

When he created the "Great White City" of glittering buildings at the World's Columbian Exposition in Chicago in 1893, architect Daniel Burnham set off a Beaux Arts explosion. Decrepit American cities rushed to remake themselves, and Washington turned to Burnham for help. Predictably, the prosperous architect, who had designed depots for the Pennsylvania Railroad, familiarly known as "Pennsy," began with a working monument to rail travel. In 1901 Pennsy President Alexander Cassatt agreed to construct a leviathan station atop the sewery remnants of Tiber Creek. Burnham's inspiration was Rome's Baths of Diocletian. "Make no little plans," he wrote. A steel frame bore the massive granite and concrete walls. Constantinian arches, egg-and-dart molding and gilt leafing, and coffered ceilings glistened in the Great Hall waiting room. The train concourse behind it became the largest room in the world; it could hold the 555-foot Washington Monument laid on its side, with 205 feet to spare. The station included a white-tablecloth restaurant, a lavish presidential suite, a reading room, a pool hall, and a bowling alley. Towering above them all were 40 massive stone legionnaires by Louis Saint-Gaudens.

By 1928, 301 trains departed daily. So jammed was the terminal during World War II that passengers reportedly bribed porters to seat them in wheelchairs so they could get to trains. The city still talks of the day in 1953 when the "Federal Express" barreled through the back wall and fell through the concourse floor. No one died, although 43 people were hurt.

The heyday of passenger-rail travel soon passed. In 1958 the railroads talked of giving away or razing the worn-out terminal, but nothing came of it. In 1968 the U.S. Interior Department worked out a deal to create a "National Visitor Center" at Union Station, complete with a multiscreen slide show in a recess gouged in the Great Hall floor. Scorned as "The Pit," it closed in 1978. So, too, did the entire building in 1981 after leaks in the roof became unrelenting and mushrooms were found growing in deserted offices upstairs.

But the nation's new passenger railroad, Amtrak, began to win riders with its speedy Metroliner service. Congress approved roof repairs, then created the public-private Union Station Redevelopment Corporation to revive the old station for travel, shopping, and entertainment. The Great Hall was set aside as "restoration space." The first crews found buckled floors and a ceiling full of holes. Everything from Saint-Gaudens's sentinels to delicate Pompeiian traceries to more than 10,000 square feet of ceiling glass panes was restored.

On September 29, 1988, the contractor pulled back velvet ropes and opened Union Station for the first time in eight years. Where there had been puddles, a pocked marble floor, and the Pit, there was again a glorious monument to the golden age of rail travel.

Switching engines pull cars to the coach yard or carshop soon after Union Station opened in 1907. By 1928 a train arrived or left Union Station every five minutes. (Leroy O. King, Jr. Collection)

Some of the ornamental lamp
fixtures appointing Daniel
Burnham's parade of classic
groin vaults in the front arcade
were lost to souvenir hunters,
but most were saved and
carefully restored.

The light-dappled West Hall,
once a ticketing and baggage-
checking alcove, is now one of
several upscale shopping
arcades. Each Christmas season,
miniature trains arrive and
depart here.

Willard Hotel

Washington, D.C.

When Abraham Lincoln slunk into town under the protection of Pinkerton guards for his first inauguration, he stayed at the Willard Hotel. Mark Twain penned two books—and Julia Ward Howe the words to "The Battle Hymn of the Republic"—there. The term "lobbying" was coined when Ulysses S. Grant humored job supplicants in a corner. Calvin Coolidge spent his vice presidency in a Willard suite. One night in 1963, Martin Luther King, Jr., sat in his Willard room and added a few lines to the speech he would deliver the next day. "I have a dream. . . " they began.

Was it any wonder, then, that an estimated 13,000 people showed up in November 1969 as the closed and leaking "Hotel of Presidents" auctioned off its furnishings and fixtures?

The richly ornamented Palm Court and Peacock Alley promenade once made the 1901 Willard the capital's most elegant address. But like downtown around it, it had turned dowdy, and its owner pleaded for permission to level the hotel. There was talk of a National Square ("Nixon's Red Square," critics sneered) on the site. But pesky preservationists, led by a group called "Don't Tear It Down," agitated; the quasi-public Pennsylvania Avenue Development Corporation put the hotel at the forefront of its plans; and the Willard was saved.

The vantage point from one of the Willard's signature bull's-eye windows is perfect for a view of monuments to two presidents: Jefferson, right, and Washington.

Washington real estate magnate Oliver T. Carr eventually won development rights. His plan mirrored the old hotel's bull's-eye dormer windows and limestone-gray brick whose thin layers of mortar gave it the appearance of stone. The city's Commission on the Fine Arts required that Carr preserve the Pennsylvania Avenue and 14th Street facades, along with both lobbies, Peacock Alley, and two public rooms, and they were faithfully restored and sympathetically refurnished. A rickety parking garage; the old, eight-story Occidental Hotel next door; and the separate Occidental Restaurant, beloved by generations of Washington politicos, fell prey to the $120 million redevelopment, but the historic Willard Hotel was back, looking as regal as ever.

Gone from the lobby are the vinyl furniture and Art Deco smoking stands of an earlier, unsympathetic renovation, in favor of restored scagliola columns, heavy red rugs, and English oak chairs.

Opposite: Peacock Alley in the newly restored hotel. Top and above: Frances Benjamin Johnston's photographs of the new Willard's 1901 opening helped restorers match furnishings. (Library of Congress, Prints and Photographs Division)

Overleaf. Almost razed to make room for an office building or a Moscow-sized National Square, the Willard was saved and restored as an anchor on the north side of a revitalized Pennsylvania Avenue.

Flagler College

Saint Augustine, Florida

Saint Augustine was the end of the line when Standard Oil millionaire Henry Morrison Flagler of New York took his second wife there for a winter's stay in 1885. America's oldest city was the railroad's last stop; south of it was a malarial bog. Sleepy, tumble-down Saint Augustine had been an invalids' wintering hole, what Flagler College history professor Thomas Graham calls "a macabre colony of people who were coughing, dying, and also playing the flute, because that was one way you could keep your lungs clear, by playing a wind instrument."

Flagler grew to know Saint Augustine while convalescing there from a liver ailment. But by the time he returned in 1885, a luxury wooden hotel, the San Marco, had opened for "strangers," as the locals called tourists, and Flagler decided to build his own "Xanadu" on spongy land that held lemon and orange groves just outside the Spanish defense perimeter walls.

Ponce de León was named after his home region in Spain, but León was "lion" enough for Henry Flagler, who had leonine stone sentinels chiseled into the his hotel's entryway gateposts.

The result was a soaring, pearl-gray concrete edifice with great twin towers and red-tile roofs. Close your eyes, a local publication suggested, and from the terra-cotta balconies so reminiscent "of a Mohammedan mosque . . . we might almost expect to hear the muezzin's call." Flagler named the hotel the "Ponce de León" after the explorer whose romantic quest for a fountain of youth brought him to Florida. Inside, the Ponce was a cascade of opulence: George W. Maynard murals, marble floors and fireplaces, Virgilio Tojetti canvases, and carved-wood paneling. The 800-seat dining hall boasted an elliptical barrel-vault ceiling, clerestory pierced with Tiffany stained-glass windows, and musicians' galleries.

In 1888 Flagler added a less haughty hotel, the Alcazar. Others put up palaces, and Saint Augustine began a short reign as "America's Winter Newport." But its decline, which Flagler's own Florida East Coast Railroad triggered by pushing though drained swamps to Palm Beach, was meteoric. Flagler would soon call Saint Augustine "dull" by comparison with South Florida and Gulf Coast resorts. The Ponce de León reported its first deficit in 1924 and would never again show a profit. On January 18, 1967, Flagler Systems President Lawrence Lewis announced that the hotel would close at the end of its 80th season and reopen as a college for women.

In 1985 Flagler College, by then coeducational, began a $22.5 million historic restoration, of which $13 million was earmarked for the old Ponce. A highlight was the reconditioning of Maynard's murals, which seeping rainwater had badly deteriorated and which someone had carelessly "repaired" by filling cracks with beige paint. During restoration the artist's signature was spotted. It read, in Latin, "Maynard made it, 1887." A special delight was the return to working order of fountains in courtyards and gardens surrounding the old hotel. In this collegiate incarnation of the Ponce de León, they are now truly fountains of youth.

Below: Courtyard of the Ponce de León hotel, now part of Flagler College, and the dining room, now a student chow hall, still graced by a clerestory pierced with Tiffany stained-glass windows and featuring two musicians' galleries and murals. Seeping rain water had severely damaged the room's murals.

Gibson Inn

Apalachicola, Florida

Sunshine—a great name for a Florida hotel, and the Gibson Inn in the panhandle coast lumber and seafood town of Apalachicola could easily have received it when sisters Annie and Mary Ella "Sunshine" Gibson bought the 1907 Franklin Hotel in 1923. Instead they lent their last name to the 31-room cypress-and-pine inn. With its two decks of wrap-around porches, wicker chairs, and tin roof, the Gibson Inn exudes tropical indolence. Its lazily turning ceiling fans and blinds with wooden slats accentuate the colonial milieu. The restless are invited to explore the cupola and widow's walk for a look through a spyglass at the oyster boats on Apalachicola Bay—or what else passes for activity. The town stirs for "Harry A's Shark Fishing Tournament" and the Saint George Island Chili Cookoff, but that's as frenetic as it gets.

Stories are served with the margueritas in the Gibson bar: of the inn's postWorld War II tenure as a boarding house and saloon, and of owner Ben Watkins's dragging furnishings out onto the lawn for a giant yard sale after a fire in the late 1970s. Guest rooms sat empty after inspectors closed the inn, and the gulf air and bleaching sun turned its vivid blue and white exterior into indistinguishable flecks of gray.

Buying the old Gibson for $90,000 in 1983 were Michael Koun—a W. R. Grace Company shipping executive from Chicago—his brother Neil, and a friend. Their subsequent $1 million restoration entailed rebuilding the veranda and cupola, both missing. Original exterior colors were copied, and a creaking grand staircase was re-created from a single surviving newel post. Period pieces like giant armoires, pedestal sinks, and four-poster beds soon filled each room. The dining room was restored to the steamboat captain's-room configuration of its halcyon days.

The Gibson reopened in November 1985, and the staff hardly broke stride when Hurricane Kate struck two weeks later. "We let the wind blow through," Michael Koun says. "We kept the bar open. It was a 'hurricane party,' all right. The *Tampa Tribune* compared it to a scene in the James Cagney movie *Key West*. The only damage was one broken window." Today a surprising number of guests are marine biologists and other professional environmentalists. Industrial runoff from as far away as Atlanta has fouled oyster beds, and the Apalachicola River and Bay are intensely studied. But even a dedicated conservationist has to rest occasionally, and one can sometimes be spotted dozing over a good book on the Gibson Inn veranda.

A 1907 photograph proved to the U.S. Department of the Interior that the former Franklin Hotel had a cupola, thus certifying the restoration and authorizing a new one for the Gibson Inn.

Timber from the banks of the
Apalachicola River, closely
copying original beams that had
decayed, was used in restoring
the hotel bar, which soon
became the scene of a
memorable "hurricane party."

Hay House

Macon, Georgia

The Hay House's massive, riveted bronze front doors, with their noble lion's-head insets, are not bronze at all. They are pine, expertly painted and weathered to look for all the world like metal.

Opposite: At dawn or any other time, the view from the Hay House cupola was the grandest in Macon. The Johnstons' Italianate "country house" stood out in a city replete with Greek Revival.

Overleaf: W. Randolph Rogers's statue Ruth Gleaning, *which can be swiveled to catch angles of light through the ballroom clerestory, was the showpiece of the Johnstons' art gallery.*

Imagine it's 1977, you're the Georgia Trust for Historic Preservation, and you've just been given the most prominent historic dwelling in central Georgia. Its 12-foot, 500-pound, silver-hinged, faux-bronze doors open to reveal a trompe l'oeil hallway, palatial rooms with detailed plasterwork, and objets d'art from all over the world. Three families lived in the 1854 house, and you want to preserve and restore it for public visitation. Which family's lifestyle and tastes do you emphasize, and to which period do you restore and interpret the house?

The answer rings clear: You restore the 18,000-square-foot, 24-room Italian Renaissance Revival mansion to all three, thinking of it as the Johnston-Felton-Hay House but calling it just the Hay House because that's how everyone in Georgia knows it.

Cotton was king in Macon, but this magnificent château was built by the proprietor of a jewelry store—albeit the largest between Raleigh and New Orleans. Following his marriage in 1851, William Butler Johnston and his bride, Anne, set off on a Grand Tour of Europe, shopping along the way for furnishings for the "country home" they would erect back home. The Italianate red-brick structure, with its octagonal stone cupola, central heat, and hot and cold running water drawn from a 20,000-gallon attic tank, stood out in a city filled with Greek Revival villas. To the right of the carved-mahogany grand staircase, visitors beheld a 50-foot-long gallery with a 30-foot clerestory and double Waterford crystal chandeliers; the room's centerpiece was—and is—a W. Randolph Rogers sculpture, *Ruth Gleaning*. Dinner guests were served near an arched, curved stained-glass window made in Vienna.

The mansion eventually passed to the Johnstons' daughter, Mary Ellen, and her husband, state legislator William H. Felton. When they both died in 1926, the house was sold for $61,500 to Parks Lee Hay, a self-described "shoestring capitalist" and art collector. Seeing the fading splendor of the house as "rather dark and dirty," the Hays remodeled and refurnished. Following their deaths, their children opened the house to now-legendary tours by Chester Davis, the Hays' longtime butler. Finally, the family donated the house to the Georgia Trust. Over a decade, the trust raised more than $560,000 for the house's revitalization, while exhibiting rooms to reflect all three owners. For instance, it interpreted a children's suite—including a mammy's room and a bathroom with half-sized fixtures—to the Johnston era.

In 1982 Maximilian Ferro of the Preservation Partnership wrote that the Hay House could emerge as "a benchmark against which we might measure comfort." The *Macon Telegraph* had reached the same conclusion 122 years earlier. It called the house the "palace of the South."

Jekyll Island Club Historic District

Jekyll Island, Georgia

Profiteers from America's Industrial Revolution who were pals at New York's Union Club had a problem, or more accurately, two annoyances and a void. The annoyances were their busy social schedules, from which they agreed they could use a respite, and the continual intrusions of reporters who exposed their excesses. The void? They had no fitting place to hunt.

To the rescue in 1885 came a member whose brother-in-law happened to own Jekyll Island, a verdant barrier cay six miles off Brunswick, Georgia. The island, on which this family had planted cotton since antebellum days, teemed with deer, boar, and alligators. Claimed by British General James Oglethorpe and named for his friend and patron, Sir Joseph Jekyll, it had been the home of Guale Indian oyster-gatherers and Spanish missionaries until Oglethorpe banished them. For $125,000, 50 Union Club members and friends bought Jekyll, incorporated, and dispatched landscape architect Horace W. S. Cleveland to lay out a site plan.

Then came the "robber barons," most aboard their yachts. Asked his *Corsair II*'s cost, John Pierpont Morgan gave the classic reply, "If you have to ask, you have no business with a yacht." The nabobs' shingle-style cabins were hardly rustic, and their Queen Anne–style clubhouse, where members were served by chefs and waiters from fine New York restaurants, was a tony party place. By 1900 hunting was out, and golf was in. Women were most welcome as guests but were banned from membership until the club's last, struggling years.

The Depression—and the new income tax—of the 1930s shoved a dagger into the Jekyll Island Club. Even opening the Club to "associate members" did not stanch its decline, and most of the idle rich simply abandoned their holdings. The last residents left under duress from military police watching for U-boats during World War II. These MP patrols—and the condemnation of Jekyll Island by the state of Georgia in 1947 following a $675,000 settlement to club members—kept the remnants of a gilded era from disappearing into looters' lofts.

Georgia placed Jekyll Island under an autonomous state authority such as the one that runs Stone Mountain. A causeway to Brunswick opened the island to development in 1954, but the deteriorating historic district was off-limits. Most plutocrats' retreats stayed bleak and boarded until 1986, when Brunswick architect F. Larry Evans and others sank $25 million into restoring the clubhouse as a Radisson hotel. "That woke us up," says the state authority's Warren Murphey. Spending about $300,000 a year, his crews began restoring cottages and club buildings like Faith Chapel for public visitation. The project will continue into the 21st century. While it lasts, Warren Murphey's crews will be turning what *Munsey's Magazine* in 1904 called "the most inaccessible club in the world" into a public preservation laboratory.

The Queen Anne–style clubhouse was the social center of Jekyll Island's yachting set. Its private restoration in 1986 "woke up" state authorities, who began refurbishing millionaires' cottages.

Saint Philomena Church

Kalawao, Hawaii

Saint Philomena Church on Kalawao, a remote nubbin of the Hawaiian island of Molokai, was restored in the late 1980s, not because of its structural merits or its unforgettable history, but because of the *person* who served there. He was Father Damien, born Joseph De Veuster in 1840 in the Flemish village of Tremeloo.

Damien was a farmer's son who had answered the Catholic Order of Sacred Hearts's call for missionaries in Hawaii. His flock would turn out to be 700 lepers, a pejorative term then freely used to describe victims of a disfiguring disease that condemned them to exile. Leprosy had devastated the Hawaiian population, and ostracism was Royal Hawaiian policy. Damien's stay among the pariahs was supposed to last three months, but he would rarely leave the colony once he devoted his life to them. Damien bathed sufferers' ulcerated bodies, comforted orphaned children, buried the dead, and worked tirelessly on the village's Saint Philomena Church. He could not know that the year he left Flanders, Dr. Gerhard Hansen of Norway had discovered the leprosy bacterium. It would be more than 50 years after Damien died in 1889—of the disease whose misery he had helped to salve—before a sulfone-drug cure would be found.

Beginning in 1987, the nonprofit group Friends of Father Damien raised $700,000, including more than $25,000 sent by Aloha Airlines passengers who had found an appeal in their seat pockets, to restore Damien's church. Artisans replaced a church wall that had been knocked down in a hurricane and crudely rebuilt, and cleaned and repainted the altar and icons. "Townspeople wanted to know why we weren't making things new," said project architect Spencer Leineweber of Honolulu. "We told them the important thing was that Father Damien had built it with his own hands. Even where wood was damaged by rot or termites, we repaired it and put it back in. We wanted to remember not a great building, but a great man."

Opposite: Before the reverential restoration, mud had oozed into the chapel, original pews had come unglued and unscrewed, and woodwork had begun to rot. Overleaf: To the right of the entrance is a lava-rubble addition built by Damien's devoted assistant, Brother Ira Dutton. Its "sanddash" walls are finished with sand thrown against wet paint.

Below: Church icons and statuary were lovingly cleaned and repainted, and red, painted lines, originally drawn to simulate brick, were restored to their original configuration.

Opposite: Lolling guests looked out at a wooden pier, extending 300 feet into the Pacific. It featured a bandstand with covered pergola, under which Hawaiian musicians strummed ukuleles and hula dancers undulated.

Top: Waikiki Beach around 1920 bore little resemblance to the sea of international humanity—and hamlet of high-priced hotels—that it would become. (R. J. Baker, Bishop Museum) Above: "Baby Moana," c. 1904. Born to a nanny and a hotel engineer, she would grow up to be silent film actress Mona Beth Rae. (Sheraton Moana Surfrider Hotel)

Kirkwood Ranch

Hells Canyon, Idaho

Every few miles in Hells Canyon, North America's deepest gorge, the roiling Snake River scoured a wide, loamy bar. There, protected from biting winds and howling snowstorms above, Nez Percé Indians fashioned winter villages and buried their dead. Later, ranchers—including Dr. Jay Kirkwood and his family, the first white squatters on the bar around 1880—took their place. In 1933, at the height of the Great Depression, ranch foreman Len Jordan, together with his wife, Grace, and a partner, bought Kirkwood Ranch, which by then included a white-frame house, a blacksmith shop, and a cabin that had been built by a bootlegger. Because Grace kept a journal that grew into the book *Home Below Hell's Canyon,* and because Len Jordan would later become Idaho's governor and a U.S. senator, the story of their hardscrabble life on the remote Kirkwood Bar would spread throughout the Great Northwest.

Grace's days were filled with canning, cooking—often for dozens of smelly sheephands—making soap from fat and lye, and caring for "bums"—not Depression hobos but orphaned lambs. The only electricity came from a clever water wheel in Kirkwood Creek that Len had jerry-rigged out of cowbells bolted to a wheel from an old Model-T Ford. Grace dealt with all manner of visitors; still visible in the Jordans' kitchen is a peg, hidden on a rafter above the stove, where Grace could grab a pistol if needed, while pretending to reach for a towel.

The Jordans left Kirkwood Ranch in 1943 for a better spread, and Kirkwood passed through several owners. In the 1970s the federal government rejected proposals to dam and flood much of the lower Snake River canyon to provide hydroelectric power and irrigation for nearby towns and ranches. Instead, noting the area's scenic attractions, Congress established the Hells Canyon National Recreation Area. The U.S. Forest Service eventually set about restoring the various Kirkwood buildings as a museum attraction beside which rafters could stop and picnic. Inside one cabin, river rangers have displayed some of Grace Jordan's canning and cooking gear. Kirkwood "is a still pretty primitive place," according to ranger Roy Lombardo. "You don't find manicured lawns and well-painted cabins out here. There were old car bodies and junked wagon wheels all around, and the dump was right out at the foot of the stream." The very coarseness of the setting, he adds, "fits this wilderness perfectly."

The Jordans disassembled, moved, then reassembled as a blacksmith shop a cabin that had been built by another early rancher who went off to World War I and never returned. Opposite: The U.S. Forest Service has turned this bunkhouse into a visitor center with exhibits on river-ranch life. Over the hill, between the fence and the mountains, is the rushing Snake River.

Old Idaho State Penitentiary

Boise, Idaho

When you walk through the first steel door into the eerie rusticated sandstone compound of the Old Idaho State Penitentiary, it's not just what you see that's important to understanding the historic territorial prison. It's who: the horse thieves, rustlers, stage robbers, and murderers whose presence you *feel*.

The *Idaho Statesman* in 1870 called the just-opened prison "the best and neatest public building in Idaho Territory." Crowded in on top of one another, 90 convicts to 39 cells, inmates were less appreciative. A 42-cell, three-tier structure added in 1890 housed the first two female inmates. Women cons would later get their own building outside the walls. On a walking tour you discover the "Black Maria," a two-cell steel cage used for solitary confinement, in which at least one inmate went certifiably insane, and another tomblike solitary-time building that the prisoners called the "Hardboil." But the Old Pen's most remarkable feature is found alongside the walkway the inmates facetiously called "Park View Boulevard." Here is row after row of prize roses, like those once nurtured by inmates seeking a scent of civility. Gone is the courtyard gallows, from which six convicted murderers were hanged between 1901 and 1926.

False stone facades had many uses over the life of the prison. Two of three survive, one being lost in a riot. Opposite: Work remains in this 1899 cellblock, where slop buckets were still in use in the 1960s. Convicts had no view of the lovely rose garden— or menacing gallows.

But it's the men and women who endured these grim surroundings who bring the Old Pen's story to life. Most notorious of all was Lyda Southard, who did time for the arsenic murders of three of her six husbands. "Lady Bluebeard" obtained the arsenic by soaking flypaper in water, then using the broth in her recipes. She escaped from the Idaho Pen and married a man named Harry Whitlock, but was recaptured. Counting his blessings, Whitlock got an annulment.

Two violent riots in the early 1970s added impetus to calls for a new prison, and by mid-1974 the last of the 13,000 convicts who had done time in the Old Idaho Penitentiary had been moved to a new, dormitory-style "correctional institution" elsewhere in Boise. Over the next six years, the Old Pen evolved as an all-too-realistic mirror of prison life. The Idaho State Historical Society, which got the crumbling buildings, stabilized them, then replaced roofs, restored catwalks, repaired sidewalks, and brought back the courtyard's magnificent roses. Today's visitors have a big edge on yesterday's cons, of course. They enter voluntarily, stay but briefly, and leave at will. And at this penitentiary, they can "come out smelling like a rose."

Chicago Theater

Chicago, Illinois

When a narrowly saved theater is not just a landmark but the "Wonder Theatre of the World," many have cause to celebrate: architects and art lovers and preservationists, for sure, but also aficionados of high finance, for they can appreciate best what it took to keep the radiant Chicago Theater, in the heart of the city's downtown Loop, from a date with the wrecking ball.

From the moment it opened in 1921, the 3,488-seat Chicago defined elegance. Its marquee flickered like swirling electric sequins beneath a soaring terra-cotta arch. Amidst the pinwheeling bulbs flashed its "CHICAGO" trademark, which advertisers and even the city would soon adopt as an informal symbol of the town. Inside was a little *palais,* replete with crystal chandeliers and fabulous objets d'art, including cloisonné Chinese vases and Carrara busts.

From 1949 to 1952, fiberglass fixtures, cheap upholstery, and false ceilings "streamlined" the theater. By 1982 it was all but abandoned, and real drama began. The Plitt Company, owners at the time, sold out for $11.5 million; a new ownership group, Chicago Theater Restoration Associates, gave the dowager theater a beautiful facelift (even a "remoisturizing" of its magnificent murals); the Illinois Landmarks Preservation Council got "conservation rights," meaning the Chicago could not be demolished or significantly altered; and city loans kept a jewel shining in a problematic neighborhood. No wonder the theater could lure Frank Sinatra for its 1986 grand reopening.

But booking and profitability troubles loomed. The city filed foreclosure proceedings, only to reconsider in early 1993 while it sought a new, not-for-profit general partner. Through it all, the beautiful Chicago played on, even landing its first long-run booking, for Andrew Lloyd Webber's "Joseph and the Amazing Technicolor Dreamcoat," in the fall of 1993.

Advertisers and even city government adopted the "CHICAGO" logo, soaring before a terra-cotta arch patterned after the Arc de Triomphe, as an informal symbol of the entire town.
Overleaf. The auditorium is far wider than it is deep, giving everyone an excellent view. The last seat in the great cantilevered balcony is only 113 feet from the stage.

Girls! Youth! Beauty! were touted, c. 1936, at the busy Chicago, which was home to fabulous stage shows, bigband concerts, and even its own symphony orchestra. (Theatre Historical Society of America Archives)

Opposite: This and an identical statue, each in its own alcove on opposite sides of the stage, were executed by Michelangelo Studios of Chicago, which had supplied all the statues at the 1893 Chicago World's Fair.

Above: In the painstaking restoration of the Chicago, a special silver leafing, covered with an oil-base gold paint, was added to highlight the already rich plaster ornamentation. Many of the ornaments had been hidden under cheap plasterboard. About 60 percent of the plasterwork had been broken off and had to be copied and replaced.

The Rookery

Chicago, Illinois

The Rookery is a magnificent mishmash. Designed by a Chicago School architect, modified by an American architectural icon, renovated by a third Chicago practitioner, and restored by yet a fourth firm, the building that was touted as an office palace—largest in the world—when it opened in 1888 is a showpiece once again.

John Wellborn Root, the imaginative but less flamboyant partner of Daniel H. Burnham, designed the Rookery as a speculative office building for a consortium of investors, including Chicago developer Edward Waller and the Brooks brothers of Boston—no relation to the clothiers. Built catty-corner to the Federal Reserve Bank of Chicago, it became a Financial District fixture. Officially the building was named the Central Safety Deposit Company Building after its principal tenant. But everyone preferred "the Rookery," a name that had devolved from a wheeling, dealing temporary city hall that once stood on the site. Root even had four crows, three of them laughing, carved into the imposts of the LaSalle Street entrance arch.

More than 80,000 square feet of plate glass in 600 windows girdled the Rookery's massive cherry-red brick and terra-cotta walls. The building's most breathtaking interior space was a dynamic central light court—a sensory starburst of marble, glazed brick, translucent glass, and serpentine stairs—that called to mind London's Crystal Palace of 1851.

In 1905 Waller opted for a makeover by avant-garde architect Frank Lloyd Wright, who cloaked heavy, dark ironwork in marble and replaced Root's electroliers with Prairie Style chandeliers. A generation later, in 1931, Chicago architect William Drummond zeroed in on the La Salle Street lobby, dividing the double-story vaulted space into two prosaic single floors. In the 1940s, as the building and its clientele crept a notch below Class A, the Rookery's owners obliterated the hallmark central skylight under a gloomy coating of paint, tar, and felt.

In the 1980s, ownership slipped into and then out of the hands of the Continental Illinois Bank & Trust Company, which was struck by sudden financial losses. In 1988 bond-futures trader L. Thomas Baldwin III and some partners bought title and announced they would restore the building and take it back to its original speculative, multitenant use. Crews upgraded every window, regilded gold leaf, replaced the tarred light-court glass with prismatic panes, and copied and added several Wright chandeliers. The estimated cost of the Rookery purchase and restoration: $95 million. What goes around sometimes comes around in such projects: One of the Rookery's new anchor tenants is Brooks Brothers. Only this one does sell clothes.

Above: Calling to mind London's Crystal Palace of 1851, Root's light court was a sensory starburst, lighted by a central skylight and glowing electroliers.

Overleaf: A serpentine oriel wrought-iron staircase rises several floors. The Rookery's original owners later had Frank Lloyd Wright simplify or cover much of the "busy" Victorian grillwork.

Covered Bridges

Rush County, Indiana

Archibald Kennedy, patriarch of the bridge-building Kennedy family, was followed in the business of making functional and decorative bridges by his son and grandsons. (Rush County Heritage, Inc.)

Back in 1986 when all the fuss started, the 19,000 or so people in Rush County in the flat corn-and-hogs country southeast of Indianapolis would have been alarmed to think there were "activists" in their midst. But there were, by the hundreds: indignant crusaders who sprang up like a summer thunderstorm in Rushville and Arlington, Moscow and Homer. When they had finished, the object of their ire—the county's three-member board of commissioners—wondered what had hit them. When their terms expired, two would lose their seats by two-to-one margins, and the other opted not to test the voters' scorn.

Why the furor? The commissioners had okayed the destruction of four of the county's six historic covered bridges and their replacement with concrete-and-steel spans. Arsonists took care of the oldest and most dilapidated, the 1873 Ferree Bridge, one night while preservationist forces were meeting. But the Ferree's fate only hardened the residents' resolve. Soon they had voted in a new board that agreed to save, restore, and upgrade all five surviving covered bridges.

Covered bridges were ingrained in the history of Rush County. Lovers had spooned on them, countless photographs had been snapped of them, and the 1924 state championship basketball team had even practiced inside the Moscow Bridge. It and the other four surviving Rush County bridges were the work of the Kennedys, one of three great Indiana bridge-building families. Covering bridges protected them from rot; but they were artistic expressions as well, and carpenter Archibald Kennedy, the family patriarch, was among the nation's masters. Painted white and embellished with vinelike wooden tendrils and decorative carved brackets beneath the roof, eye-catching Kennedy bridges resembled country cottages.

The bridge lovers scored one success after another. A bridge festival and bluegrass jamboree grew into an annual event that draws tourists from as far away as Chicago. County teenagers, who had turned Offutt's Ford Bridge into a graffiti-scrawled eyesore, joined in a bridge-painting party at the invitation of two grandsons of 1940 presidential candidate Wendell Willkie. Restoration began. Workers replaced metal roofs and warped clapboard siding, and poured gallons of epoxy into loosened joints and rotted timbers. But in sound bureaucratic tradition, they ignored most of Kennedy's decorations. That didn't sit right with Jim Irvine, a covered-bridge aficionado who has built several bridge models. He climbed a ladder at Offutt's Ford Bridge and painted the faded imprint of the Kennedy signature anew—as well as recarving and replacing Kennedy's distinctive "K" pattern in the crown of each archway.

Cars and trucks and tractors still rumble across the picturesque covered bridges of Rush County, demonstrating that historic structures can be a useful part of day-to-day life.

Top: Inside the Moscow Bridge, the double Burr arch frame combines vertical, diagonal, and arched timbers for bracing. Note openings at the top that let light into the long bridge. (Rush County Heritage)

Above: Two weeks after vandals torched the Ferree Bridge, Rush County Heritage President Larry Stout reflects on the damage. (Geoff Witt, Shelbyville News)

The Kennedys often installed lattice ventilators or windows, such as this in the Offutt's Ford Bridge, to bring a wisp of light to the long dark interiors.

Indiana Roof Ballroom

Indianapolis, Indiana

It's not even a room with a view, but the city of Indianapolis and developer Melvin Simon & Associates spent $6 million to restore the Indiana Roof Ballroom. The "Roof," as it's fondly known, mixes a "touch of old Spain" with the glittering, gliding days of ballroom dancing and big bands that played the room four nights a week in the 1920s, 1930s, and 1940s.

At the Roof, on the top floor of the lavish 1927 Indiana Theatre Building, every farmer could be Fred Astaire, and each housewife Ginger Rogers, dancing beneath the (electric) stars to the music of Tommy Dorsey, or Dorothy Lamour, or Indiana favorite Charlie Davis. For years after a local band, the "Kings of Tempo," opened the room on September 2, 1927, fewer than 25 tables surrounded the "plaza." Couples came to dance, not sit and talk. Alcohol was banned, and even corsage boxes were checked for contraband; ginger ale and Bubble-Up were the offered libations, but more than a few flasks can be seen on the floor in souvenir photographs of the day.

The penthouse fantasyland featured balconies and serenading towers, faux-.tile roofs and grapevines, and even real—but stuffed—pigeons. Not just stars appeared in the dark blue "sky" above; so did "clouds," projected onto the ceiling. During World War II, when it seemed as if half the city's dancers were off fighting, the Roof struggled. It hung on for 30 years as a makeshift convention center and meeting room but finally closed in 1976. Since the theater below had folded earlier, the entire building was in jeopardy. The city bought it and turned it into the new home of the Indiana Repertory Theatre, but the Roof would sit empty for eight more years while developers came forward with renovation proposals. Finally the city awarded a long-term lease to Simon & Associates, which promised to reopen it as a dancing and banquet facility. Simon crews replaced floorboards warped by dripping water, hand-painted faded stenciling, replastered gargoyles, and coated the glazed ceiling surface with a rough acoustic foam for better sound amplification. They also added a new "scene machine" for still moodier sky effects, including synthetic "snowfall." Even the pigeons got a thorough vacuuming.

Soon the Roof was jumping again. Devotees of ballroom dancing from as far away as Saint Louis streamed in for Sunday night swirls, and to gawk, and to remember.

Dancers trip the light fantastic at the annual Eli Lilly & Company spring dance at the Roof, c. 1947. An illuminated sign reminds them which dance step fits the music. (Alice Hendricks Leppert) Opposite: Like a great opera set, the Roof Ballroom's Spanish courtyard was a plaster fantasyland of balconies, towers, and fake-tile roofs. All were scraped, repainted, or recoated in the restoration. Overleaf: Dances drew the limelight, but the Roof, now as always, stays in business as a meeting and small-convention space. Note the floor, made of maple 1 × 3's bent into an ever-widening oval.

Aalfs Manufacturing

Sioux City, Iowa

If you've ever cleaned out a filing cabinet and found a wonderful old document stuck between the drawers, you'll appreciate the story of the Aalfs Manufacturing building.

Aalfs makes Baker brand overalls and jeans for other labels. In 1976 the company decided to move assembly operations from its old building in downtown Sioux City to an industrial park. Then the unexpected happened. Says Aalfs Executive Vice President William A. Rodawig, "I pulled open a file cabinet one day, and underneath were two envelopes. On them was a drawing of our building from 60, 70 years ago. It was absolutely beautiful. I thought, if we could get it to look like that again, why would we want to go move into something much less, for twice the price?" Research turned up a photo of the five-story sandstone building with a stunning cast-iron and glass facade covering its bottom two floors. The city sealed the decision to stay by upgrading or moving out neighboring skid-row gospel missions and junk shops.

The Aalfs structure had been built in 1890 by an eastern syndicate that had come to Sioux City when the onetime trading post of the Sioux Indian Nation was booming as a processing center for Iowa corn and hogs, and cattle from neighboring Nebraska and South Dakota. Aalfs Paint and Glass Company, founded by Nittert Aalfs, and the Baker Company, makers of bib overalls and denim shirts—hot sellers in America's breadbasket—moved into the building during the second decade of the new century.

In 1939 one of Aalfs' sons bought the Baker Company. Within a few years the renamed Aalfs Manufacturing Company was cutting and sewing denim goods and, later, "baking" permanent-press chemicals into jeans. After Bill Rodawig found the envelope, rethought the building's merits, and decided to stay put, restoration began in 1983. Work crews removed storefront brick and put back the show windows. They painted the ironwork and wood trim a striking dark green to match flecks of color found on basement windowsills. Inside, behind a dry wall, they found and reopened a grand oak staircase. Restoration architects Bahr, Wermer and Haecker of Omaha also designed a two-story atrium lobby that shows off its cast-iron columns. The restoration cost Aalfs Manufacturing $600,000, roughly half the price tag of a nondescript new building.

"Our people love it here, and our customers can't believe it," says Rodawig. "In a quiet way, it tells them here's a company that's been around a long time, survived, and is doing well."

Aalfs Manufacturing's original logo—like this one from the envelope that helped save the old building—came from the days when the "House of Quality" sold paint, wallpaper and glass.

During restoration, the
distinctive plate-glass storefront,
interrupted by cast-iron
columns, was re-created. It had
been replaced by brick facing
and aluminum jalousie
windows in a 1948
"modernization."

Van Allen and Son Building

Clinton, Iowa

All roads do not lead to Clinton, on the eastward breast of Iowa, but the transcontinental railroad did, and John D. Van Allen, a courtly traveling representative for fine dry-goods houses of Chicago and New York, took the train there often. When Van Allen opted to go it alone in 1892, he chose this orderly Mississippi River town in which to open a mercantile store. Celebrated Chicago School architect Louis H. Sullivan, too, stopped in Clinton often on his way to Cedar Rapids, where he was designing a bank building. It stood to reason that when the merchant and the master architect crossed paths in 1913 just as Van Allen and his son decided to expand their business into a new four-story "House of Fashion," Sullivan would get the commission.

The building was classic Sullivan: horizontal ribbons of glass and brick interrupted by dramatic vertical terra-cotta mullions topped with a cornucopia of green leaves and brown stems. Inside, the store was all business. Chandeliers and prismatic-glass display windows threw light directly onto the Van Allens' fine linens. Aisles were wide for browsing.

Van Allen and Son prospered well into the 20th century, but specialty shops and suburban malls lured away its upper-crust clientele. In 1968 the store was leased to a chain, and for 20 more years it survived as an all-purpose outlet with a pink and lavender "South Seas" motif. The store closed in 1987, and for two years stood empty and ravaged by water damage; city officials talked of buying and demolishing it as part of downtown "beautification."

To the rescue came a distant knight: Crombie Taylor, former director of the Institute of Design in Chicago and one of America's foremost Louis Sullivan scholars. Taylor had seen the Van Allen while traveling about, photographing Sullivan's bank buildings. In a comparative flash, he and his wife, Hope, sold their houses in England and California, moved to Clinton, established a Van Allen Foundation with two friends, and persuaded the city to buy the building (for $250,000) and lease it (for 80 cents a year for 50 years) to the foundation for use as the Louis H. Sullivan Center for Learning and Louis H. Sullivan Museum and Community Center.

A $500,000 restoration, paid for by grants and donations, brought back Sullivan's terrazzo floors and mahogany paneling. Miraculously, 10 of the store's discarded mahogany showcases were discovered in places as diverse as a Clinton motorcycle shop—and donated back to the Van Allen Foundation in time for the building's 1991 grand reopening. Today, its gift shop and tea room are popular gathering places, and this farming town that has gravitated to riverboat gambling for entertainment has even come to enjoy tributes to a dead architect.

Inset among the flora at the base of each batonlike mullion is the Van Allen's distinctive VA trademark against a deep-blue background, suggesting the family's Dutch heritage.

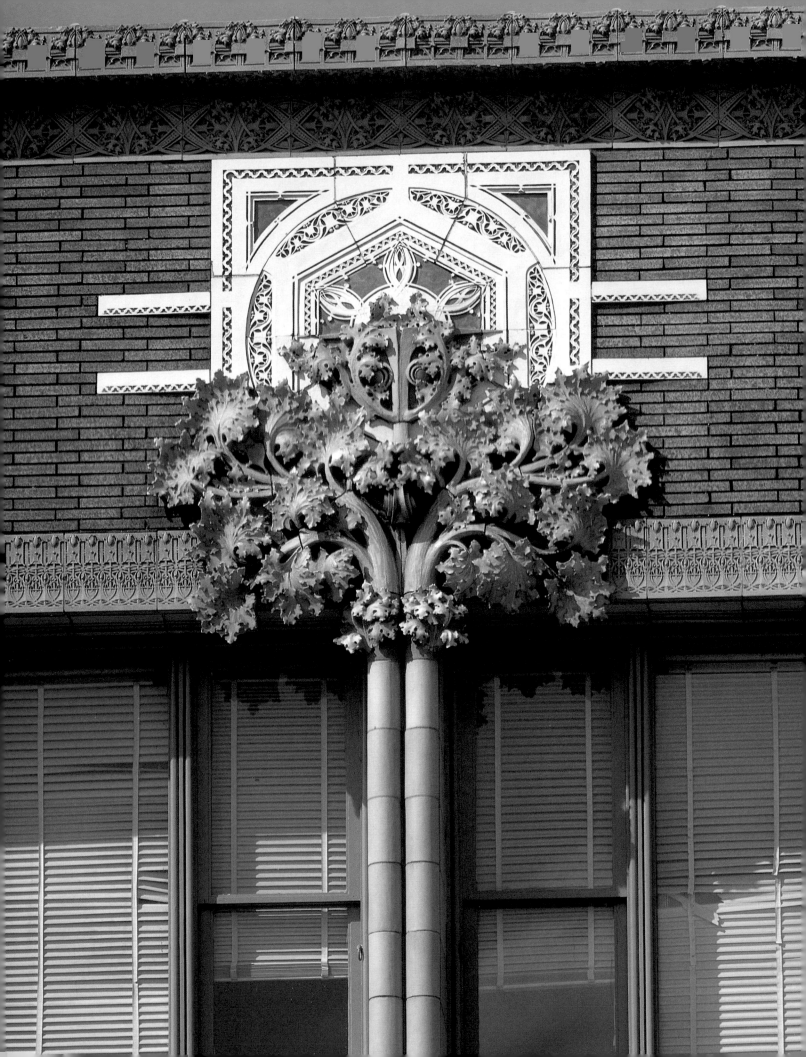

Opposite: Sullivan interrupted the store's horizontal ribbons of brick and glass with vertical terra-cotta mullions, topped with a cornucopia of leaves and stems that suggests growth and a bountiful harvest.

Above: This historic view of the store shows a distinctive window treatment. At street level, one entrance led straight to the Van Allen's men's shoe department, so farmers did not have to mix with the ladies looking for linens. (Clinton County Historical Society)

Big Brutus

West Mineral, Kansas

Sunflowers and a sea of wheat you'd expect in Kansas. A pony express station, perhaps. But unless you've really done your homework, there's no way you would be ready for Big Brutus.

Rearing like a colossal mechanical praying mantis 16 stories above the cornfields, there it is: Brutus—11 million pounds of strip-mining shovel. Brutus, which tore away one square mile of Kansas countryside each year, hoisting rock and dirt "overburden" 101 feet in the air and dumping it into trucks 150 feet away. So powerful were the surges of current when Brutus revved its engine that they dimmed West Mineral's lights two miles away.

Busy carving into a 35- by 75-mile seam of bituminous coal in 1962, the Pittsburg and Midway Coal Company (P&M) of Pittsburg, Kansas, placed a $6.5 million order with the Bucyrus Erie Company of Milwaukee for the world's second-largest electric shovel (the largest being a 20-story-tall Bucyrus Erie model operated in southwest

Rotating 360 degrees, Brutus could lift a load of rock and dirt 101 feet in the air and dump it 150 feet away.
Opposite: The Big Brutus Museum's executive director, Vicky Johnson, is dwarfed by the 11-million-pound beast. Each of the pods in the tanklike tread weighs a ton.

Kentucky). Mine superintendent Emil Sandeen dubbed the behemoth "Brutus." One look tells you where the "Big" came from.

For 11 years it roared, 24 hours a day, seven days a week. But even Brutus could not stand up to economics and government intervention. Demand for high-sulfur coal declined, and Brutus had developed a gargantuan oil leak. The Environmental Protection Agency began adding to strip miners' cost by requiring them to reclaim the land they had scarred. In April 1974 Brutus was turned off and left to rust. For 10 years P&M tried to sell the dinosaur but could find no buyer. With liability-insurance costs rising as trespassers broke down fences to climb on the old wreck, the company decided to cut up Brutus and sell it for scrap. But instead, in 1984 it agreed to donate Brutus and 16 surrounding acres to Big Brutus, Incorporated, a new, nonprofit corporation dedicated to saving the metal monster and turning it into a tourist attraction.

"Sunday volunteers" went to work, welding broken parts, stripping away the soot from vandals' fires, and repainting Brutus the old black and bright orange—but leaving its engine silent. On July 13, 1985, 10,000 people showed up for its rededication. Since then the display has grown from a card-table operation into a museum, complete with a mining exhibit. In a country full of memorials, there is none quite like Brutus, looming in the Kansas cornfields as a reminder of mechanization's awesome, and sometimes destructive, power.

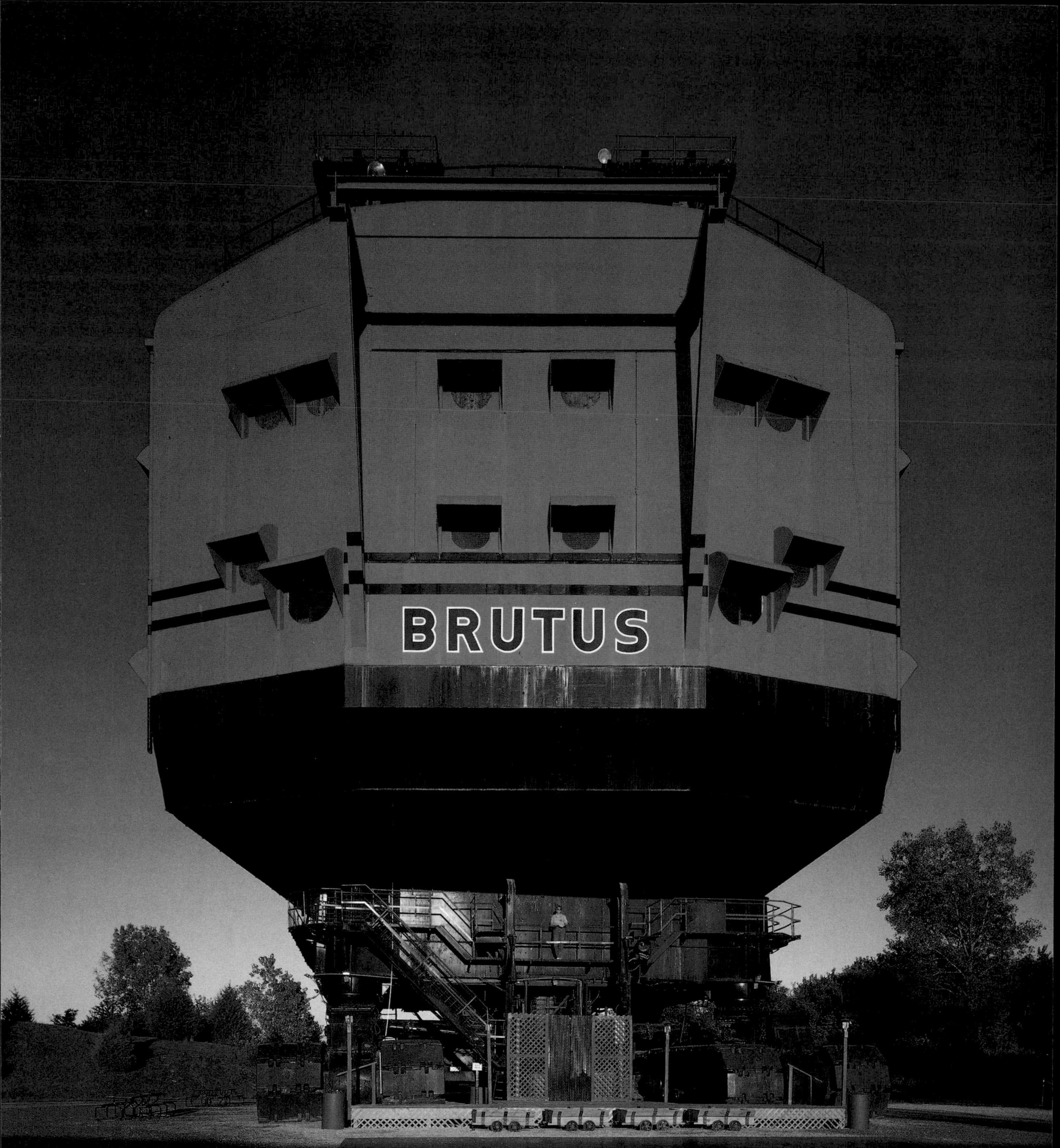
BRUTUS

Seelye Mansion

Abilene, Kansas

Kansas's Tara was built with the considerable profits of a snake-oil salesman. Just before and after 1900, Alfred B. Seelye's medicine wagons fanned out into 14 states, where his drummers would tout his "Wasa-Tusa" cure-all, "Ner-vena" nerve medicine, "Fro-zona" ointment, and even sheep dip—all concocted in a factory next to his Abilene home.

Actually, two homes. A fine Victorian structure rose in 1896, six years after "Dr." Seelye had come to Abilene from college, where he studied medicine but never got a degree. In 1904 his determined wife, Jennie, packed the family off to the World's Fair in Saint Louis to get some up-to-date ideas, then commissioned a fine Georgian manor on the same site as the old house. The new $50,000 Seelye Mansion boasted 11 bedrooms, a Tiffany fireplace in the grand hall, light fixtures personally chosen by Thomas Edison at the fair, and 18 closets.

The patent-medicine business—and the family fortune—dwindled with the advent of food and drug regulations, income taxes, and exposés about patent nostrums. As daughters Marion and Helen, who had inherited the house, aged, they received frequent offers for the tattered Seelye Mansion. Each was rebuffed. But Terry Tietjens, who owned a recreation resort in northeast Kansas, broke through and, in 1982, purchased the house. He also "adopted" Marion and Helen, then 85 and 86, with the assurance that they could stay for life.

Even fire that damaged the mansion did not dampen Tietjens's enthusiasm. He went through with the purchase and a $200,000 restoration. With financial help from his twin brother, he repaired the roof and windows, replaced fire-damaged woodwork, and found identical tin sheeting for the ballroom ceiling.

Terry Tietjens then made another change that the reclusive Seelye sisters surprisingly came to enjoy. With pride in its place as a palace in a cow town, he opened the house to tours.

Ever the wise businessman, A. B. Seelye (front row, third from left) planted his father in the center of the front row to give his snake-oil salesmen an air of respectability. The elder Seelye had nothing to do with his son's venture.

Above: Steers, driven to the stockyard, rumbled freely past one of the finest houses between Kansas City and San Francisco. To preserve its majestic profile, Jennie Seelye ordered electric and telephone cables buried.

Right: Everything from sheep dip to talcum powder left the factory on the Seelye house grounds. Note the Seelye cookbook and, twice again, Grampa Seelye's authoritative mug.

Frontier Nursing Service

Wendover, Kentucky

At heart a mountaineer, blue-blood Mary Breckinridge rode into Kentucky's poorest hollows to train nurse-midwives. (Caufield & Shook, Louisville)

Mary Breckinridge was a woman of breeding and privilege who, riding alone on horseback, combed the craggy hollows of backwoods Kentucky by day and night in search of women to train as midwives. Sophisticates called her a do-gooder, but the women of Leslie County, Kentucky's poorest of the poor, called her a friend and, in more ways than one, deliverer.

Daughter of an Arkansas congressman who served as Grover Cleveland's minister to Russia, she lived and studied abroad. But it was her childhood visits to her great aunt's estate in the Hudson Valley of New York that drew her to a Kentucky she had never seen. Grandmother Lees, as everyone called her great aunt, told of her father's Kentucky upbringing before his service in the paltry Confederate Navy; and of her grandfather, Kentuckian John Cabell Breckinridge, a U.S. vice president and the Confederacy's last secretary of war. Grandmother Lees would read letters from the plain-speaking Kentuckians the old woman was putting through college. "I realized," Breckinridge would write, "that I am at heart a mountaineer."

Married and widowed young, she lost a beloved son to a sudden illness, and then an infant daughter. Hoping to save other children, she took nurse's training in New York, and later in France and Great Britain. She saw the benefits of midwifery in France. But French midwives were not nurses, and American nurses were not midwives. She found the ideal melding—nurse-midwives—in Britain, and set off to find and better train Kentucky's "granny women."

On one of her rides she spied a beautiful hillside where she would build the headquarters of the "Kentucky Committee for Mothers and Babies." "Wendover" would grow into the nation's foremost program of nurse-midwifery: the Frontier Nursing Service, which she would direct, even after breaking her back in a riding accident, until her death in 1965.

Wendover's main chestnut-and-oak log house was erected on a geological fault, so that over the years it not so much settled as dropped, cracking walls and buckling floors. (Living room square dances did not help the situation.) In the 1980s the nursing service began a thorough restoration—replacing and caulking logs; updating wiring, plumbing, and kitchen cabinets; and supplanting a crude fiberboard roof with fire-retardant wood shingles.

As of mid-1993, the Frontier Nursing Service had delivered approximately 12,500 babies since 1951 and not lost a single mother in childbirth. The service is supported by prestigious institutions from as far away as Cleveland—and, inspired by the vision of Mary Breckinridge on horseback, reaching out to the mothers and babies of the Kentucky mountain wilderness.

Home and headquarters, Wendover was built on a fault below a spring, leaving restorers in the 1980s to deal with cracked walls, buckling floors, and rotted timbers. Nurses and couriers rolled up the living-room rugs for square dancing. Breckinridge, who had broken her back in a fall from a horse, watched with delight but could not join them.

Shakertown

South Union, Kentucky

And then there were nine: just nine Shakers left in the United States in early 1993. A century earlier, thousands of followers of Ann Lee, their charismatic founder, had flourished in communal settlements from New England to western Kentucky. The Shaker settlement at South Union, near Bowling Green, was one of Kentucky's first tourist attractions. Travelers came to see the Shakers clap loudly, sing, and dance, with hands cupped to receive God's love or shaking downward to rid themselves of evil. One of the early onlookers was President James Monroe.

Residents lived as celibate brothers and sisters. If an existing family joined the sect, the parents were assigned to different families, and the children were raised by other Shakers. Trustees conducted business with "The World." Shakers dressed humbly and revered simplicity—as captured in their song that goes, "'Tis the gift to be simple. . . . " But they welcomed phones, electricity, and the latest farm machinery. They were mocked for their pacifist beliefs, especially at South Union, where suspicious slaveholders harassed them.

Since Shaker men and women could produce no offspring, converts and orphans whom communities took in were expected to swell their ranks. Instead, older members died, young men left, and not many newcomers joined. The agrarian societies withered, and by 1922, South Union was no more. Its 4,000 acres were subdivided and sold. The central part of the village evolved into the South Union Shaker Museum, nurtured by a nonprofit group called Shakertown Revisited. It restored the main "Centre House" to its 1840s appearance, including white plaster walls, woodwork painted with mustard and fish oil, and trademark peg rails adorned with original Shaker brooms and chairs. Donations and foundation grants covered the $350,000 cost. The effort exemplified the Shaker motto: "Put your hands to work and your hearts to God."

Made of bricks fired in the community kiln and standing on a 10-foot-high, smoothed-limestone foundation, the 1824 Centre House was a dormitory for Shaker stalwarts.

In this c. 1885 photo of Shaker leaders, women are wearing silk kerchiefs made at South Union, and the men are in their "Sunday finest." (Shaker Museum at South Union)

Grinnan Villa

New Orleans, Louisiana

Henistory almost robbed Henry Howard, designer of more than a score of great Louisiana houses, including the Madewood, Nottaway, and Belle Grove plantation manor houses, of credit for one of his most gracious creations: the 1850 Grinnan house in New Orleans. Nathaniel Cordlandt Curtis in 1933, for instance, called it "the finest in the Garden District" and chalked it up to James Gallier. Even the soaring Belle Grove usually is attributed to Gallier.

One reason might be that, whereas Gallier built as well as designed—and therefore collected far fatter fees and greater notoriety—Howard, trained as a carpenter in County Cork, Ireland, somehow survived on design commissions alone. He finished the Grinnan place in less than seven months, a point the present owner delights in pointing out to his architect, whom he chides for taking five years to restore the house 140 years later.

No doubt the late Greek Revival home stood out in what was then a rowdy section of the flatboat port of Lafayette, one of the first American suburbs of French New Orleans. Perfectionist Howard's specifications called for mortar made of "well burnt Thomaton lime and clear Natchez or Horn Island sharp sand," the "best Northern white marble accurately cut." The Grinnan house featured a one-story portico with the obligatory exuberant Corinthian columns in a design that could be (and was) easily confused with Gallier. Howard may have been "practicing" for his plantation designs by creating a house that is delightfully asymmetrical, starting with a front door that is off center. The current owner's 1987–92 restoration brought back the house's original center-cut pine floors, which had been obscured by parquet oak flooring about 1910; duplicated two interior Corinthian columns whose footprints were discovered in the entrance hall; and copied Howard's original honeysuckle-design ironwork after the company that had produced it was found to be still in business and in possession of the original molds.

The restoration architect, Barry Fox, says the result is a "museum-type" restoration, a villa that Henry Howard, now given proper credit, would know to a tee. Regrettably, whereas Robert Grinnan took his last breath as a wealthy man, Howard died poverty-stricken and alone, of paralysis, in New Orleans's Charity Hospital, where, ironically, he had designed the new syphilitic wards and dissecting rooms.

Henry Howard made perhaps the "finest [house] in the Garden District" deliberately asymmetrical. The grounds included a greenhouse, poultry house, stable, and extensive servants' apartments. Opposite: Howard was a master at building sturdy foundations in New Orleans's soupy soil. This alcove, overlooking the garden and croquet court, was the only spot that had settled after 140 years.

Parlange Plantation

New Roads, Louisiana

Louisiana's effervescent history has been enlivened by many legendary families. But only one, the colorful Parlanges of Pointe Coupee Parish, has managed to hold onto a plantation homestead from the days of 18th-century French land grants until today, and their raised French Colonial home is the largest of its type remaining anywhere in the United States.

When the Marquis Claude-Vincent de Ternant built his plantation house in 1750 on land granted by the French crown, the task and terrain were daunting. He chose a snake-and-mosquito-infested thicket of brambles, live oaks, and magnolias 120 miles up the Mississippi River from New Orleans civilization. But he made do, erecting a West Indies–style house of cypress and bricks that slaves made from bousillage—a mix of Spanish moss, deer hair, and mud. Walls rose above a raised basement, with tapering columns made of wedged-shaped brick (later covered with stucco) below, and slender cypress columns above. The upper columns supported a wraparound *galerie* and a steeply pitched hipped and dormered cypress-shake roof. French doors and windows, hung beneath delicate, fan-shaped transoms, opened in front toward what is now False River—a 22-mile horseshoe-shaped lake that, in the marquis's day, was part of the Mississippi where the channel doubled back on itself. Beside the entry road, M. de Ternant also built octagonal, two-story pigeonniers, which would become Parlange's trademark.

The family history turns enchanted when told in the Creole lilt of "Miss Lucy" Parlange, the sixth-generation mistress of the plantation. On her tongue, "Vincent," for instance, becomes the proper French "vass-*saw*." Miss Lucy, her husband, Skipper, and their son, Brandon, undertook a wholesale restoration of Parlange, beginning in 1980. Brandon says, "It was hard for [workers] to understand we were more interested in preserving the high-quality, virgin cypress than cutting out the old and throwing it away." Crews stripped the gallery and interior floors by hand, using steel wool, and repainted the exterior in original colors. Brandon Parlange also turned the upstairs of one of the pigeonniers into a guest room. Today, the Big House is filled with eclectic antiques and stunning paintings, including the life-sized portrait of the estate's Civil War–era mistress, Virginie de Ternant, completed in Paris.

At Parlange on a foggy morning, you can look out through the moss that's swaying in the live-oak trees like a diaphanous figure. Some swear it's a ghost, but Miss Lucy tells them the only ghost at Parlange is the Holy Spirit. If you're lucky, she'll bid you stay for one of her "bannister brunches" on the gallery. She says, "We believe it when the Bible says, 'You never know when you welcome strangers; you might be entertaining angels unawares.'"

Opposite: A life-sized portrait of Virginie Parlange dominates the parlor. A child's portrait hangs in the corner—of Julie de Ternant, Virginie's daughter. Overleaf: More than a few apparitions have been sighted amid the Spanish moss in the live oaks that line the lane to M. de Ternant's West Indies–style cypress-and-brick plantation house.

Norlands

Livermore, Maine

Talk about family dynasties! Consider the seven Washburn boys: governor of Maine; secretary of state under Ulysses S. Grant; minister to Paraguay; U.S. senator from Minnesota; Maine banker; member of the U.S. House of Representatives from Wisconsin; U.S. Navy captain. (Their parents, Israel, Sr., and Patty Washburn, also had three daughters, whose exploits, not surprisingly for the times, were less well documented.) Like lottery winners or athletes who've signed fat contracts today, the Washburn sons, as they "made it," wanted to thank their elderly, blind father and their even more inspirational mother, who had died. So, in 1865, they went together to enlarge and remodel the family farm home, only to see it burn to the ground; they then commissioned an Italian-style villa with a wraparound veranda from which the assembled Washburns could reminisce and enjoy the family at play. Son Charles gave the estate its name during a blizzard, quoting Tennyson's *The Ballad of Oriana:* " . . . loud the Norland whirlwinds blow."

So numerous were the Washburn heirs that, when the father died, a cumbersome timeshare arrangement had to be devised to determine who could use the property when. Eventually little used, the mansion and its outbuildings deteriorated and, in 1973, were deeded to the Washburn-Norlands Foundation, which began a fascinating "living history" program in which visitors leave behind almost every vestige of 20th-century existence and step into the arduous life of an 1870 Maine family. While guests churned butter, thrashed hay, and cleaned bedchambers, the foundation undertook a $1 million restoration of the house, library, and community church. Today a stay at this working farm gives people much to experience and even more to later appreciate as they return to their easier, though not necessarily better, lives.

The seven sons of Israel and Patty Washburn were all great successes. Left to right, they are: Algernon, Elihu, Cadwallader, Israel, Jr., Charles, William, and Samuel. (Washburn Norlands Foundation Archives)

*Norlands is now a "living
history" center, in which visitors
leave behind the vestiges of
20th-century life and, briefly,
step into the arduous world
of a Maine family in 1870.*

Third Haven Meeting House

Easton, Maryland

In 1985 Maryland's oldest known building was about to become its latest old building to collapse. The 1684 Third Haven Quaker Meeting House on the serene Eastern Shore sagged, canted, and showed evidence of rot along the foundation. Whole rafters were hollowed by termite damage and fragile as a rice cake. In 1985 the Society of Friends, wishing to save their historic structure, began raising the $50,000 they thought would be needed to restore the rickety building. It would take six years and nine times that amount of money before the job was done.

Independent-minded Quakers were early settlers of the Eastern Shore, across the Chesapeake Bay from Baltimore and Washington. The sect derived from England, where its founder, George Fox, had challenged civil and religious authority with the unorthodox ideas of his Religious Society of Friends. Hauled into court in 1650 for preaching against the Church of England, Fox admonished the judges to "tremble at the Word of God." One of them promptly branded Fox and his followers "Quakers," and the name stuck.

On Maryland's Eastern Shore, the Quakers built settlements and formed "meetings" (congregations). Carpenter John Salter was commissioned to build "ye Greate Meeting House" in a dense oak grove on Tred Avon Creek. On October 24, 1684, the first service was held in the simple cruciform wooden building. Nameless at first, it was eventually called Third Haven. No one's sure why; perhaps as a corruption of "Tred Avon."

In Quaker fashion the meeting house was bisected by columns with panel dividers. (The sexes worship together, although they sit on opposite sides of the room; when matters pertaining to just the men or just the women are discussed, the partitions are closed.) William Penn and George Fox were among the early Quakers who spoke (or perhaps just reflected) at Third Haven.

In 1794 members widened the building by demolishing the cross wings and extending the rafters on one side only, giving it a distinctive, lopsided saltbox appearance. After 1880, when a brick meeting house was constructed for weekly worship, the old structure was used less and less; it stood for another century in increasing disrepair. In the 1985 long-postponed restoration, termite-damaged downstairs rafters were saved by pumping them full of epoxy. Work crews removed the 1939 roof and replaced its cedar shingles with new ones. They braced, bolted, and gusseted weakened attic rafters to tie the building together and prevent sagging.

Faint, scribbled messages can be seen on the wall along the attic stairs. One, signed by "Robert Reushat, 1782," reads, "Gone but not forgotten." Had the Third Haven Meeting not finally acted to save the venerable meeting house, that could easily have been its epitaph as well.

To look at the asymmetrical meeting house on a serene cove on the Tred Avon now, you'd never suspect it was once near collapse from rotted and termite-infested timbers. The saltbox shape is reminiscent of many early New England homes.

Boott Cotton Mill No. 6

Lowell, Massachusetts

The Boott's bell summoned thousands of "Lowell girls" to their looms, signaled their breaks, and gave them leave to go home.

Opposite: The work, threading the looms, checking fibers constantly to be sure they did not twist or break, and changing bobbins and shuttles, was difficult, dangerous, and deafening.

Lowell was once a city of bells. But not church bells. Starting at 4:10 A.M. and tolling at intervals throughout the day and evening, these were the bells of the six giant mill complexes crowded along a one-mile stretch of the Merrimack River. By the thousands, "Lowell girls"—young women ages 14 to 30 from the rocky farms of New England—rose, trudged to work, hurried back to their dormitories for breakfast and lunch, quit at the end of their 13-hour workdays, and were summoned to church on Sundays to the peal of those bells.

Chelmsford, as Lowell was first known, bloomed as America's first planned industrial city thanks to a sly industrial spy. While vacationing in Great Britain in 1811, Francis Cabot Lowell of Boston dropped in on Manchester's textile mills. Forbidden to take notes, he turned his remarkable photographic memory toward each detail of the turbines and clacking looms. Lowell and his partners then opened a mill in Waltham, Massachusetts. In 1823 operations shifted to Chelmsford on the rushing Merrimack. Lowell was dead by then, and Chelmsford was renamed for him. Overseer and part-owner Kirk Boott ran the largest Lowell mill complex. Three-fourths of its 2,200 workers were women, happy to get the $3.25 a week wage, less $1.25 for board. One worker, Lucy Larcom, wrote in 1889 that the weave room's deafening noise became a silence to her. "Its incessant discords could not drown the music of my thoughts."

Lowell declined precipitously after World War II, as mill operators succumbed to Tennessee and the Carolinas' allurements: nonunion labor, inexpensive land, ice-free rivers, and tax incentives. Boott shut down in 1954; its largest building, No. 6, hung on as a Wang Corporation warehouse. In the 1970s Lowell's superintendent of schools, Patrick Morgan, floated the idea of turning Lowell into an "educative city" of industrial museums and heritage trails. Politicians won funding for a new, federally sponsored Lowell Historic Preservation Commission, Wang sold Boott No. 6 to the commission for $1, and the National Park Service began restoring it as a monument to the Industrial Revolution.

Inside as part of the $20 million restoration, the National Park Service in 1986 re-created a functioning weave room by purchasing 88 Draper looms then still in use in Tennessee. The $20 million restoration required the rebuilding of 522 mostly broken window frames. Private developers of other Boott buildings ran aground on the severe New England recession of the 1980s, and their projects were foreclosed by their New York City bank. Even so, once-forlorn Lowell had become Patrick Morgan's "educative city," with Kirk Boott's old Mill No. 6 as its centerpiece.

Cobblestone Farm

Ann Arbor, Michigan

Draw a line westward on a map from the old Ridge Road across northern New York State, then across southern Ontario, and it leads to Michigan's lower peninsula. Thousands of Irish masons who had helped carve the Erie Canal out of solid rock took that route, finding work building fireproof farmhouses out of glacial stones that Michigan farmers were unearthing. One of the most creative among them, Stephen Mills, was picked to build a cobblestone addition to Dr. Benjah Ticknor's tiny wooden farmhouse in Ann Arbor—population 3,000—in 1844.

Ticknor was a navy surgeon who had served all over the world. He had sent his brother Heman to purchase land in the newly opened Michigan Territory, and Heman built a small wood-frame house on 183 acres. Finding their new home full of nieces and nephews when they finally beheld their new home in 1840, Benjah and

The Campbell family, c. 1903, relax on the porch. Three generations of Campbells worked the 225-acre farm and kept the cobblestone house essentially unchanged for 91 years. (Cobblestone Farm Association)

his wife, Gesie, set Mills to work on a Classical Revival cobblestone house, with the stones on the front facade arranged in the distinctive herringbone pattern of the day. Inside, tulipwood walls and doors were "grained" with faux knots and whorls; and hand-worked laths, timbers, and nails were employed throughout.

The farm was sold at Dr. Ticknor's death in 1858, and again in 1881—this time to William Campbell and his wife. Three generations of Campbells would live there for the next 91 years. Grandson George Campbell and his sister, Mary, eventually sold most of the estate for development and lived in the house until they sold it and four-and-one-half surrounding acres to the city of Ann Arbor in 1972. Their Cobblestone Farm, as it was known, became the last piece of a 43-acre city park. In 1974 five citizens, outraged at the loss of Ann Arbor's historic masonic hall, formed the Cobblestone Farm Association, which over the next 16 years would raise more than $150,000 to stabilize and restore the old cobblestone house. Included in the work were the replacement in kind of a rotted cedar-shingle roof and the addition of authentic period furnishings—including a melodeon, Chickering piano, rope bed, and candlewick bedspread.

Cobblestone Farm visitors today can encounter costumed 19th-century characters like chair caners and tole (enameled metalware) painters. Often a balloonist even floats overhead. Blessedly, there's something more than another tract of ranch houses to look down upon.

Light and shadow added an eastern refinement to Stephen Mills's herringbone cobblestone pattern, in which oval stones projected from the wall, and mortar was formed into a V shape.

Geldner Sawmill

Cleveland, Minnesota

In 1973, the year it was shut down, there was not much left to recommend the once-thriving Geldner Sawmill.

Running diagonally through Minnesota's Land of 10,000 Lakes are the "Big Woods," a 20- to 60-mile-wide band of deciduous hardwood maple, basswood, ash, hackberry, box elder, and various nut trees. It was into the Big Woods that thousands of sawmills set up shop in the 1860s and 1870s, feeding the demand for timber for houses and fishing and hunting cabins. One mill, between Jefferson and German lakes, belonged to Prussian immigrant Charles Heckert. It ran for 103 years, the last 67 under the ownership of Leonard Geldner and his son, Leo.

From the Geldner Sawmill came railroad ties, wagon-makers' boards, and coffin lumber for the state hospital in Saint Peter. Until 1947, when the state condemned it, a basement steam boiler, fed by wood scraps from the cutting process, powered the Geldner mill. Thereafter, a large Minneapolis tractor, parked outside the door, supplied the power to turn the 54-inch blade. Because of family illness and decreasing demand for rough-hewn lumber, the Geldners shut the mill for good on December 3, 1973. The machinery sat rusting as wooden walls and flooring warped and bowed, miraculously escaping fire and vandalism.

In 1975 James E. Hruska, and his wife, Dorothy, who was president of the Le Sueur County Historical Society, were driving along County Road 13 when they became intrigued by the old sawmill. After long negotiation, Le Sueur County had itself a sawmill for $9,000. In a $150,000 restoration, contractors dismantled the rickety structure and rebuilt it, using extensive original lumber, including the main support timbers that Charlie Heckert had hewn by hand. Restoration coordinator John Zimmerman, the county parks chairman, went to work with other volunteers on the once-condemned boiler and on the engine.

Then came the decision not just to display, but also to demonstrate, the old equipment on Sundays and holidays from mid-May to mid-September. On October 17, 1982, at the dedication, the mill's whistle blew for the first time in nine years. At one time, every one of Minnesota's 87 counties had a sawmill like the Geldners'. "There's nothing unique about the design or layout or function of it," says John Zimmerman, "except for one thing. It's the last one left."

Above: Back in operation for summertime Sunday demonstrations, the mill is run by volunteers, some of whom worked in sawmills that once proliferated in Minnesota's Big Woods.

Overleaf: The 54-inch saw blade, removed so its teeth can be sharpened, is turned by belts (more dangerous than the blade) connected to a 145-horsepower engine below ground.

Longwood

Natchez, Mississippi

Longwood is the "Unfinished Symphony" of American historic restoration. The stunning antebellum home — the largest octagonal house still standing in America — has not been brought back to the splendor cotton nabob Haller Nutt intended when he put northern craftsmen and plantation slaves to work building it. And so long as the Pilgrimage Garden Club of Natchez owns it, it never will be.

Instead, Longwood is a freeze-frame testament to the demise of an opulent era when Natchez boasted 11 millionaires—more per capita than any city in America. Dr. Nutt was one of them. With the firing on Fort Sumter and the spasms of rhetorical venom against all things Yankee, the Philadelphia artisans who were building Longwood put down their tools and fled north while the fleeing was good. They had completed only Longwood's exterior; 24 inside rooms remained undone.

Disheartened but not yet daunted, Nutt turned his crew of slaves toward completing the basement as a temporary living quarters. But because Nutt, like many wealthy planters, had opposed secession, the Rebels burned his crops; then the Yankees stole every window frame, mantel, and chimney cap piled outside Longwood, and made off with the wagons and livestock. In 1864 Haller Nutt died a broke and broken man.

His widow, Julia, and their children hung onto the octagonal brick "Oriental villa," surmounted by a "Persian dome." They survived for a time eating weeds and drinking soured milk. "It's a *Gone With the Wind* story, only much more fascinating," says Mimi Miller of the Historic Natchez Foundation. Longwood stayed in the family until 1968, when Kelly E. and Ina May McAdams of Austin, Texas, bought the house and four acres and, through their foundation, donated the estate to the Pilgrimage Garden Club of Natchez, with the understanding that Longwood be preserved.

Today, walking through Haller Nutt's Longwood, admiring some of the few furnishings—Haller's gout chair and the breeze-inducing mahogany *punkah* fan over the dining-room table among them—one can hardly imagine the primitive, haunting scene of abandonment above. There, still exposed to the elements through uncompleted arch windows, Longwood's rusted paint cans, discarded tools, and never-completed woodwork are a ghostly symbol of the finality of war.

Yankee artisans almost literally "dropped everything" to flee north when the Civil War broke out. Broke and broken, neither Haller Nutt nor his widow could ever afford to finish the work.

*Nutt's stunning "Oriental villa"
was well on its way to becoming
the talk of moneyed Natchez.
Gingerbread moldings and
interior shutters were
concessions to Mississippi tastes
and climate.*

Manship House

Jackson, Mississippi

Mississippians who graciously show off their renowned magnolia-draped mansions take extra pains to point out a humbler workingman's house. It was crafted over 11 years, beginning in 1857, on what were then the outskirts of their new capital city. Its owner, Charles Henry Manship, was a prosperous paperhanger, ornamental painter, and trustee of the insane asylum. He would be elected mayor of Jackson and appointed postmaster by his friend, Confederate President Jefferson Davis, holding these positions, as he later wrote in pencil in his memoirs, "until driven out by Yankee Bayonets." Behind those blades came Union General William Tecumseh Sherman, to whom Mayor Manship surrendered the city on May 14, 1863. While the mayor's home escaped the scourge, Sherman left much of Jackson a smoldering "Chimneyville."

Manship had *walked* to Jackson from Vicksburg. He quickly gained a reputation as an artistic painter through his work on the rising Mississippi Capitol, and his paint and wallpaper shop flourished. When it came time to build a fine house, he drew inspiration from a drawing in A. J. Downing's book, *The Architecture of Country Houses.* But Manship's olive-and-cream Gothic house would be made of pine, so ubiquitous in Mississippi, not Downing's favored stone. Inside, he applied his own painted marbling and graining to fireplaces, doors, and trim.

After Manship's death in 1895, the family lived in the house for four generations as downtown Jackson grew up around the site. In 1975 Jackson's Junior League and a number of individuals, including the state's first lady, Carroll Walker, convinced the legislature to purchase the Manship House and grounds. The price was a modest $110,000, but $600,000 more would be needed to restore and shore up the house, whose wraparound porch had sagged nine inches into Jackson's oozing clay. A highlight of the restoration was the detail work of English wood-grainer Malcolm Robson in the faux-oak dining room.

The emphasis at the Manship House is on a workingman's everyday life. Rugs have tears, and floors are unshined in the fashion of the times. Today, in addition to welcoming tourists, the house marks a special occasion once every five years: a Manship family reunion.

Mayor Manship's olive-and-cream Gothic Revival residence was raised on pilings and studded with 10-foot windows to catch every possible wisp of air in Jackson's sweltering summers. Opposite: Handyman Manship left his initials on the window cornice to the left in the master bedroom. Wallpaper was another Manship specialty; this is a reproduction of the original.

Bollinger Mill

Burfordsville, Missouri

Developers have been a part of the nation since the Revolution and before. George Frederick Bollinger, a North Carolinian who served as a major in the American army along the Mississippi River after the Revolutionary War, was one. Bollinger struck a deal with the Spanish commandant of the portion of the North Louisiana Territory now known as Missouri. He was awarded a 640-acre land grant on a promontory called Cape Girardeau, on condition he develop the land and bring more settlers. Bollinger returned to Carolina, fetched six of his brothers and their kin—and 14 other families—and headed back to Missouri.

He got busy constructing a dam on the Whitewater River, a mill made from logs, and a distillery. The Bollingers accumulated great wealth, largely on the backs of slaves. During the Civil War, federal forces shelled, but did not completely destroy, the mill. The family sold out to Solomon R. Burford, and by 1870 the settlement, which Burford renamed for himself, had grown to include blacksmith and cooper shops and a "liquor shop" called The Hop Tea Joint. From 1895 to 1953, the mill was one of three owned by the Cape County Milling Company, which produced the popular Gold Leaf flour until huge competitors like Pillsbury put it out of business. In 1953 the mill site was sold to the Paul Vandivort family, who, ironically, were descendants of the Bollingers. In 1961 they donated it to the Cape Girardeau County Historical Society. Six years later the property was turned over to the state, whose Department of Natural Resources has operated it as a state historical site since that time.

Sharing the site is the Burfordsville Covered Bridge, once a profitable toll bridge for the Green Road Company and now one of four remaining covered bridges in Missouri. Begun in 1858, the 140-foot span is buttressed by the "Howe construction" system, in which vertical iron rods draw the diagonal wooden members tight against the top and bottom of the bridge.

In restoring the site, state crews replaced beams under the mill's first floor that had been eaten by termites, as well as 80 percent of the yellow poplar flooring damaged by leakage and floods; they also gave the covered bridge a new roof to replace one torn off in a tornado.

In the mill's salad days, says Gary K. Walrath, the state parks division's assistant regional supervisor, a well-paid specialist rode a circuit, "dressing" mills' grinding stones by removing high spots and recutting the grooves. "Bits of metal would come off the drill and catch in his arm," says Walrath. "You could judge a millwright's experience and diligence by how much his arm was cut up. That is where the expression 'a man worth his metal' comes from."

Below: Once powered by a giant waterwheel, Major Bollinger's mill later was driven by a turbine to grind grain. Union troops burned part of the mill in the Civil War, but it was rebuilt.

Bottom: Because of fire danger—and to ward off rats and snakes—mills are kept as clean as possible. The Bollinger Mill still grinds small quantities of meal for visitors to buy.

Ruskaup-Niewoehner Stone House

Bay, Missouri

Mummified mice above a false ceiling, and a front porch held together with rusted Missouri license plates dating to 1929 were not promising harbingers of Harry and Joyce Niewoehner's dream place in the country. The limestone-rubble house in Gasconade County looked more like a moonshiner's cabin than the historic German farmhouse, built by immigrant Heinrich Ruskaup, that it turned out to be.

The 1845 house incorporated many typical German, but also French and American, touches. It had a long porch, dormers, and a fireplace; most rural German cottages were straight-line houses heated by more practical stoves. Signature features were the low doorways and heavy butternut or white walnut doors with raised diamond panels. The attic was used to store wheat, which had to be lugged up the stairs. When the Niewoehners' carpenter pulled down the first-floor board ceiling, grains of wheat—as well as the embalmed mice—tumbled out.

The day was dark and snowy when the couple first looked over the abandoned, disheveled house in 1965. Stepping onto the porch, Harry fell through a "floorboard" of rusted license plates. Inside, the couple found no plumbing, and the fireplace was covered with an old panel door. There were five or six layers of peeling wallpaper in every room and linoleum on every floor, and the rusty metal roof that had been tacked over shakes 40 or so years before was curled and flaking. Floors elsewhere sagged. "I told Harry we'd be crazy to buy this," Joyce says.

But they took the plunge and bought the Ruskaup House in 1977, and the Niewoehners and their son, John, spent more than a decade's worth of weekends and short vacations restoring it. Underneath the wallpaper, they found original stenciling, which Harry reproduced throughout the house. They installed a new shake roof and crafted wooden storm windows.

"This house is our Hawaii or Virgin Islands," Joyce Niewoehner says. "What you see in this house are our trips, our vacations." The farmhouse, which they furnished with a walnut rope bed, rag rugs, an old Missouri pine cradle, and a wood-burning kitchen stove, is exactly the cozy place in the country that the Niewoehners sought. They keep eyeing the property's dilapidated barn, which could well be their next "vacation" destination.

In 1914 brothers Ben (left) and Chris Ruskaup walk their prize mules down the state road that separated their house from the barn. The road later became U.S. 50 running across the entire nation.

*A walnut rope bed, old
Missouri pine cradle, and Harry
Niewoehner's careful reproduction of Heinrich Ruskaup's
antebellum stenciling highlight
the cozy master bedroom.*

Custer County Art Center

Miles City, Montana

Miles City was born in 1876 as a rowdy ragout of whiskey peddlers, fur trappers, and prostitutes, and named for Lieutenant Colonel Nelson A. Miles, the officer who ordered the riffraff to camp two miles distant from his army cantonment. But culture was quick to get a foothold once the railroad arrived in 1881, and waves of homesteaders followed after 1900.

A cosmopolitan prairie town needed a water system, and in 1911 city engineer Grover C. Pruett was commissioned to create a waterworks complex outside of town. The water plant was a pragmatic structure of red brick and reinforced concrete with a hip roof of asbestos shingles. It performed reliably for 63 years before being replaced by a modern facility in 1974.

A loftier function than water treatment—the display and dissemination of art— was just getting a foothold in Miles City at the time. "Big Sky" artists abounded, but there was no good place to exhibit or sell their work. The old pumping station was considered, but it was so full of dials and pipes that it simply would not do. Then someone pointed to a manhole cover leading to the waterworks' gigantic underground settling tank. Could it be . . . ? The unlikely bunker did have long expanses and few obstructions; it was well insulated, beneath the sod, against Miles City's fierce climate extremes; and the price, $10-a-year rent to the city, was right.

Soon the deal was done, and the new Custer County Art Center's board was off raising restoration funds. The center has since mounted eclectic exhibits, including life-size mud and straw horses and a large "road kill coyote." "We do have some avant-garde exhibits," agrees Executive Director Susan McDaniel. "On purpose." No longer does such art have to be underground. Yet of course, owing to its setting in Grover Pruett's old settling tank, it does.

The same walls and columns that rose from this incomplete 1924 expansion of the Miles City water plant can be seen in today's underground art center interior.

Below: The Custer County Art Center has an unusual entrance canopy. The gallery's location—snug inside a Yellowstone River hillock—keeps it delightfully climate controlled.

Bottom: You'll find more than cowboy art inside the art bunker. With excellent acoustics, the cavern has hosted a variety of musical concerts, meetings, and orations.

Depot Center

Livingston, Montana

Despite the mountain attractions of the nearby Absaroka Range, the lore of western adventurers, and all of the ranches that fill the valley, Livingston is a railroad town to its core.

Pushing west on the new main line to Tacoma, the Northern Pacific Railroad reached the area in 1882. Livingston soon would be home to the Northern Pacific's "helper engines" needed to nudge trains over Bozeman Pass, as well as the system's vast locomotive maintenance shops. The city lay 50 miles above Yellowstone, the nation's first national park, and Northern Pacific posters soon touted the "Route of the Yellowstone," referring to the river as well as the park.

In 1910 the railroad commissioned Charles Reed and Allen Stem—architects of New York City's Grand Central Station—to give Livingston a three-story, Italianate terminal with terra-cotta adornments, two annexes, and wrought-iron stairs. Walls were built of buff-colored Chinese bricks that had once been used as ballast in transoceanic ships. Inside and out, the railroad's red and black "yin-yang" logo, which an executive had seen on the Korean flag at the 1893 Chicago World's Exposition and adapted, appeared in profusion.

Soon well-heeled travelers streamed in, en route to Yellowstone. Livingston boomed, but could not sustain its growth when the automobile opened Yellowstone to direct access; rail passenger service declined; and the Burlington Northern (BN), into which the Northern Pacific had merged in 1970, gradually phased out the locomotive shop. By the early 1980s the depot's delicate mosaics had been painted a gaudy "BN green," and locals remember using the virtually abandoned station as a Halloween haunted house. Burlington Northern offered the depot free to Livingston in 1985, and a group of citizens agreed to help turn the dingy old eyesore into a community arts center. Over the next two years they would raise $800,000 for a wholesale restoration in which Seattle architect David Leavengood redesigned the interior for exhibits.

For its first six years, the refurbished Depot Center mounted western-theme exhibits. But the collection expanded to include Northern Pacific "Streamliner" displays, featuring artifacts and art pieces donated by Burlington Northern President Gerald Grinstein. Once again the Livingston Depot had become, vicariously, the nostalgic hub of grand Vista-Dome rail travel.

Part of the Depot Center's new emphasis on railroadiana is a nostalgic display of artifacts from the golden days of travel on the Northern Pacific's "North Coast Limited" and other sleek trains. The Northern Pacific's "yin-yang" logo is a telltale sign of the railroad that turned Livingston from a dusty speck on the western landscape into a bustling rail center.

Dowse Sod House

Comstock, Nebraska

About four miles from the tiny town of Comstock, population 60, stands a remarkable house built in 1900 and made of "Nebraska marble." This material, quarried right out back in the bottomlands of the Middle Loup River, is good, old-fashioned Great Plains sod—tufts of coarse bluestem grass clumped in rich soil and held together by its intricate web of roots.

Lacking enough trees to build a house, homesteaders like 29-year-old William Ryan Dowse improvised. He sliced long, four-inch-deep strips of sod with his "grasshopper breaking plow," cut them into 30-inch "bricks," and stacked them grass side down in rows that became the walls of his prairie home. Precious two-by-fours were laid across them to form joists and an attic outline. More sod was arranged atop the roof paper, and window and door openings were cut. Finally, muslin was tacked to the joists to make a dirt-catching false ceiling.

As his cattle farm prospered, William Dowse topped his house in cedar shingles and added a pine floor and a porch to house the cream separator. All the outbuildings, including a windmill and a sod chicken house, were blown to bits in a 1941 tornado, but the soddy stood undamaged.

The house stayed in the family, but after son Bill and his family moved away and his brother Curt, who bought the farm, tore down fences, cows broke down the soddy's doors and took refuge from the sun. The Dowse house would surely have disintegrated—as did thousands of other soddies as families surrendered to locusts, prairie fires, blizzards, droughts, epidemics, Indian attacks, and homesickness—had not family members and neighbors accepted a challenge from another son, Philip, to help restore it. One of many jobs was a complete interior replastering, using the old-time material made from sand, clay, and hog's hair. There are some gaps in the sod: "Those are crowbar holes," Philip says with a wink. "In a storm, my parents would stick a crowbar through them. If it came back in bent, they wouldn't venture out."

Travelers who wind their way through the Nebraska sandhills and cornstalks, 40 miles from the closest interstate highway, and don't go too fast down Custer County Road s21c, may spot the handmade sign near Comstock that points down a road to the soddy. What they'll find there is one of America's finest restored examples of a classic "Little House on the Prairie."

The Dowse house became fancy as soddies went. Not only did it have a side porch and cedar-shingle roof, it also got a cement coat in 1935 to keep it from washing away.

William Dowse and his bride, Florence, went to a photographer's studio in Burwell to have their wedding photo taken in 1900. They have the grim look of settlers with a hard life ahead.

Farmers Bank & Trust Company

Nebraska City, Nebraska

Nebraska City—Tree City, U.S.A., the home of Arbor Day—used to be where the action was. Nebraska Territory's first capital, a teeming meatpacking center, and the site of Fort Phil Kearney on the Oregon Trail, it was bigger than Omaha in the 1880s.

No wonder the United States Post Office Department in 1888 was bamboozled into building a Richardsonian Romanesque post office that was far larger than the town merited. The red "butter brick" post office, which the town newspaper pronounced "a daisy" with the "most perfect" steam-heating system "ever invented," was a 23,000-square-foot version of a ubiquitous government design. Even if the $105,000 building's second-floor offices were used for the ladies' library association and not the hoped-for federal courtroom, it was a gem.

Nebraska City wangled itself an overblown "butter brick" post office by exaggerating its population. Well into the 20th century, its lobby was a social gathering place, even on Sunday after church.

Opposite: The Marcottes, who restored the bank, kept the best of the old postal facility, such as cast-iron radiators that wrap around columns and the riff-sawn oak supporting columns and oak-and-glass screens.

Except for stories about holdups and a big paint job, the post office got little more press until it closed in 1986. A few blocks away, Arvon Marcotte, president of the Farmers Bank & Trust Company, had been eyeing the building as a possible new headquarters for his booming bank. His was the first—and only—bid. It was rejected. But a later $50,000 bid was accepted.

Restoration of the bank became a family affair. While professionals patched the stonework and reroofed the building, Arvon, his wife, Lu, and their children stripped woodwork, stained and varnished floors, plastered walls, hung wallpaper, and polished marble. The Marcottes, who were careful to keep the circular cast-iron heat radiators that wrap around columns, ordered linoleum, government-issue temporary partitions, and other nonoriginal building fabric removed. They brass-plated the radiators and turned them into check-writing stands, and stripped the 15-foot, oak-and-glass screens that had surrounded the original post office boxes. A new teller counter and partial partitions repeated the screens' ornamentation.

The Marcottes discovered a secret that not even most Postal Service employees knew: Above the clerks' cages was what looks like an air vent. Instead, it was really a peephole through which postal inspectors would spy on workers. Not exactly a secret, but easily overlooked, is the old post office's third floor, where the Marcottes found discarded fixtures. Soon they were wondering: Wouldn't an in-town loft apartment above an old bank building be fun?

Fourth Ward School

Virginia City, Nevada

In the boom-to-bust history of Virginia City and the Comstock Lode, 1875 was a record bust year. Silver mining was suspended in the Sierra Nevada town—named after a prospector, "Old Virginny" Finney—after a market crash in San Francisco sent mine stocks plummeting to a fraction of their inflated worth. Worse, a character known as "Crazy Kate" knocked over a lantern in a barn, igniting a fire that would level two-thirds of the town in less than a day.

But the "Richest City on Earth," then at its apex of about 20,000 gold- and silver-bewitched souls (the permanent population is now around 700), rebuilt with a vengeance. Along with Piper's grand opera house and a lavish county courthouse whose Statue of Justice was appropriately constructed without a blindfold, up went a grand new Empire Style schoolhouse, the Fourth Ward School. Architect C. M. Bennett's massive new three-story building, whose unusual diagonal sheeting gave it strength against the area's howling "Washoe zephyrs" off Sun Mountain, cost $100,000—a staggering amount for the times.

The school dutifully served the community until the 1930s, when a shrunken Virginia City struggled to weather its own depression. As part of the federal Works Progress Administration program, workers in 1936 built a new high school, and Fourth Ward closed and was turned into a storehouse. Three times over the next three decades, citizens got together to save it from collapse and out of the hands of developers. Finally, in several stages from 1984 through 1986, a wholesale restoration as a museum and community center was completed, paid for by grants and more than $150,000 raised by another citizens' committee.

The weight of the schoolhouse's roof pressing down on the "balloon" structure—in which single 32-foot Ponderosa pine studs extend all the way from the masonry foundation to the roof—had caused the sides to bow outward. To solve the problem, crews bolted a series of large posts and beams through the wooden structure to the masonry foundation. They also attached studs to floors and the building's membrane with steel tie straps. "Our structural engineer called and said that the building cannot stand up," recalls restoration architect Ted Fuetsch. "We said we'd better recalculate, because it's 100 years old and still here." Fuetsch says quick, cosmetic fixes are not the answer for endangered historic buildings like the Fourth Ward School. "There's an old proverb: The ox is slow, but the earth is very patient. These buildings are very patient. They don't need our help this week. If we can study and move slowly and do only what is necessary to pass them on to the next generation, we have done our part."

Majestic as the dreams of the silver miners who built it, the Fourth Ward School is extra sturdy. Bracing and diagonal sheathing have kept it upright in the face of howling winds.

Million-Dollar Courthouse

Pioche, Nevada

Pioche, named for Francois L. A. Pioche, a San Francisco financier who formed the Meadow Valley silver-mining company but never set foot in his namesake settlement, is a western tumbleweed town that wouldn't die, mostly because it had the good fortune to be a county seat. Otherwise, this remote, parched town of 400 hasn't much more to commend it than a girls' school, a prison honor camp, and a few gaming tables. The silver mines played out long ago, but tiny Pioche does have a curious tourist attraction: its "Million-Dollar Courthouse."

In 1872 Lincoln County moved its government offices from Butler and Pearson's Saloon into a fancy new courthouse that would eventually make Pioche the laughing stock of Nevada. The structure was a 40-by-60-foot Italianate building with a separate jail out back. Initial cost projections put the courthouse at $16,000 and the jail at $10,000.

When it was new, Pioche's sturdy new courthouse and jail dwarfed the simple homes and miners' shacks that surrounded it a half-mile from town. (Lincoln County Museum Board)

Changes in the courthouse design and build-now, pay-later financing soon ballooned costs, so that by the time the job was done in 1878, the tab had hit $75,000. The county dallied on its payments, and by 1890 the obligation had hit $450,000; by the time the debt was finally retired in 1938, no one had any idea how much had been spent, and the legend that the modest little complex had become a "Million-Dollar Courthouse" may not have been far askew. In a monograph on Lincoln County's history, James W. Hulse estimated the total at $800,000.

To add insult to injury, the courthouse started coming apart immediately. By 1935 bricks had loosened and floors sagged. A mining rebirth in lead and zinc gave revenues enough of a boost that commissioners authorized a new Art Deco courthouse that opened in 1938. The Million-Dollar Courthouse was virtually abandoned, its furnishings left to mildew.

In the 1870s a Las Vegas casino tried to buy the building and move it to the Strip as part of a "Frontier Village." Aroused and deciding they'd rather not part with their relic, area residents obtained a $171,000 federal grant to fix the most severe damage. A decade later, commissioners asked the county museum board to take over the old courthouse. Armed with two more grants totaling more than $200,000, contractors and citizens replaced the sheet-metal roof, tightened loose bricks, and retrieved or replaced old furniture. Volunteer Tom Draper contacted a Boulder City, Nevada, man who agreed to create life-size dummies of a sheriff, judge, lawyers, and jury for the courtroom—and even donated four of the figures.

With "court" back in session more than a century after the Million-Dollar Courthouse was built, Pioche, a could-have-been-ghost town, has its centerpiece back.

Bricks for little Pioche's ex-
travagant Italianate courthouse
were shipped from England all
the way around Cape Horn to
California, then hauled by
wagon across the desert.

Frye's Measure Mill

Wilton, New Hampshire

Frye's Measure Mill's delicately turned maple and fruitwood Shaker boxes come in sets of 13. Overleaf: Before it became a "measure mill," the 1817 mill housed a "carding and fulling" operation. Farmers brought in wool for cleansing and disentangling (carding) and thickening (fulling).

In the days of the general store, New England customers bought flour, nails, bulk grain—even oysters and clams—not by weight, but by volume. Every store had a set of dry-measure containers and piggins—wooden dippers with handles, used to fetch water or carry kitchen scraps to the hens and little "pig-ins." This lively demand was a boon to Daniel Cragin, who, for 50 years until 1909, ran one of America's few "measure mills" alongside Mill Brook near tiny Wilton. Cragin became so successful that he bought several lathes and metalworking machines so that he could replace his own belts and broken machine parts. For another 51 years, Edmund B. Frye, and then his son Whitney, ran the renamed "Frye's Measure Mill," adding ice-cream freezers, apple and lettuce crates, and colonial "pantry boxes" to the line.

In 1948 Harland Savage, a carpenter looking for part-time winter work, went to work for Whitney Frye. Within four years he was managing the mill, and when Frye died in 1959, Savage bought the mill from the estate. Years later his son Harley, who had studied to be an oceanographer and artist but elected to come home to Wilton, joined his father in the business, and today Harley and his wife, Pam, own it and an attached gift shop that sells the coveted Frye Measure Mill lacquered boxes. The mill is still turning out dry measures and piggins as well, forming and pressing the hardwood pieces exactly as Daniel Cragin and the Fryes had done it.

"Restoration here is an everyday event," Harley Savage says. "A millwright is always crafting new parts in the machine shop or removing and oiling and restitching these big leather drive belts. There's no place to go for spare parts." Look at the finished measures crafted the old-fashioned way, he says, "and you'll see proof-positive that they really don't make 'em like they used to."

Mill owners, left to right: Daniel Cragin, c. 1875; Edmund Frye, c. 1910; and R. Whitney Frye, c. 1920. (Wilton Historical Society)

Opposite: At these and other benches, craftsworkers make and repair molds; bend and shape thinly peeled, soaked wood into containers; and add pegs, brads, and handles.

Above: Now as in decades gone by, the work area is unheated. In New Hampshire's bitterly cold wintertime, workers follow the sun from room to room and task to task.

Strawbery Banke

Portsmouth, New Hampshire

People who would enjoy a Williamsburg-like rendezvous with America's pre-colonial past, complete with storied houses and authentic period crafts and furnishings, will certainly find it in Strawbery Banke. But in many ways a Mr. Goodbar candy wrapper from the 1940s better tells the tale of this restored city neighborhood in historic Portsmouth.

The area was first settled by Englishmen who, while sailing up the Piscataqua River in 1630, spied a thicket of berries along the west bank, stopped and ate some, and stayed to build homes and a trading post. They called the place Strawbery (with one "r") Banke. By the 1950s Portsmouth's South End had become a wretched slum, redlined for urban renewal. Fortunately, the Portsmouth Historical Society had already been at work rescuing structures, and, in 1958, another nonprofit organization, Strawbery Banke, Inc., was able to gain title to dozens of venerable homes, shops, and gardens and begin creating the "neighborhood museum" of today.

Which brings us to the Mr. Goodbar wrapper. In addition to its many early-American restorations, Strawbery Banke has ventured into the new curatorial world of 20th-century Americana. Its staff has cataloged a fascinating collection of consumer products—Ipana toothpaste, Duz soap, Regent cigarettes, even "Victory Hairpins" from World War II—for the reopening of W. S. Abbott's 1940s "Little Corner Store." Every item, down to a 1944 Mr. Goodbar wrapper brought in by inveterate collector Charles E. Burden of Bath, Maine, gets a tag that lists the date of accession, the giver, and where he or she obtained the item. "Whether it's a candy-bar wrapper or a priceless 18th-century chair, we don't discriminate," says registrar Carolyn Parsons Roy. Anonymous donors, though, are discouraged, because each item requires a deed of gift, signed and countersigned—an impossibility when the donor is unknown.

The provocative result of Strawbery Banke's sweep across the American centuries is a moving tableau that begins before Samuel Marshall's crafting of a redware bowl on his potter's wheel in 1736 and carries through W. S. Abbott's ringing up of a Mr. Goodbar bar in 1944.

Opposite: Strawbery Banke's gardens of many periods are designed to help visitors interpret total neighborhoods, when herbs and vegetables were integral to daily life. Overleaf: Two houses along "Puddle Lane": the Federal-style Lowd House (left), a cooper's residence from c. 1810, and the English colonial Sherburne House, built as a counting house, c. 1695.

Visitors who venture into Strawbery Banke expecting a colonial village are also delighted to find several 20th-century Americana displays, including this 1950s kitchen.

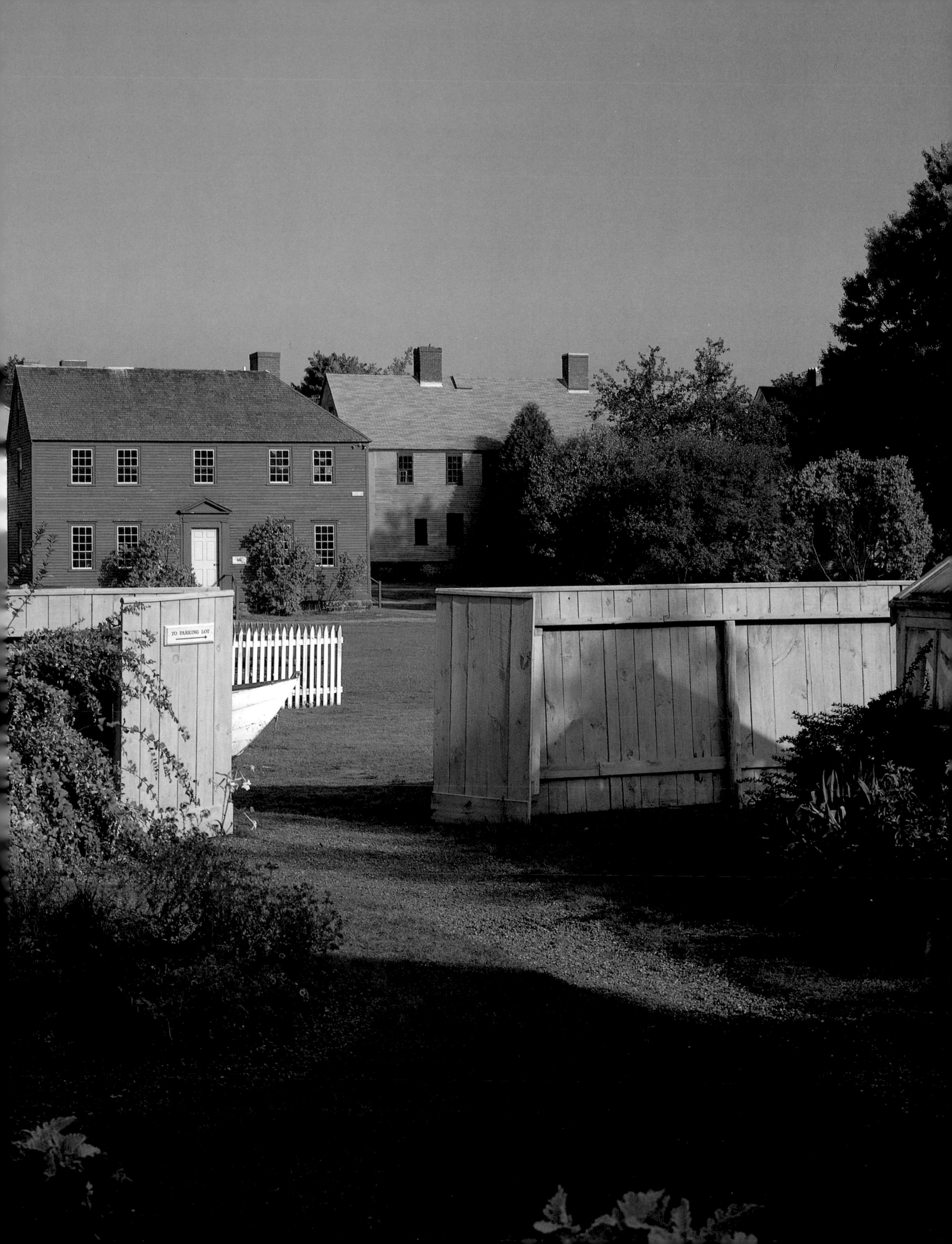
TO PARKING LOT

Emlen Physick House

Cape May, New Jersey

Gingerbread was all the rage in seashore Cape May when bachelor physician Emlen Physick, Jr., built his new, and rather strange, 18-room home for himself, his mother, and his maiden aunt in 1879. Its designer, architect "Fearless Frank" Furness of Philadelphia, preached the importance of "honesty" in buildings—letting structural framework show clearly rather than hiding it. Furness chose a radical style for the Physick House in which forms and roof lines are asymmetrical, dormers are oversized, a grid of raised board "stick work" overlies the walls, and corbeled chimneys appear to be upside down. Furness authority George Thomas speculates that the top-heavy chimneys may playfully represent a locomotive's smokestack, since Furness had designed railroad stations and worked around trains.

Ironically, the Stick Style, as it would be called, is not "honest" at all, for, unlike a Tudor house, in which beams are also visible, its stick pattern is purely decorative, and the support structure cannot be seen. Inside, the house was dim and stuffy, since Physick's mother, whose deportment was likened to Queen Victoria's, preferred the house kept at 80 degrees year-round. Dr. Physick is remembered for sporting the shore's first auto—a Packard—and for his love of animals. There is a dog to be seen in almost every photograph of the man.

Emlen Physick, Jr., died at 59 in 1916, of acute indigestion. The house passed through several hands. In the 1960s, when its owners moved to California and left it empty, it began a pathetic decline; vandals picked at it, and passersby ridiculed it as the town's haunted house. Developers bought the blighted house in 1967 with the idea of turning it into a restaurant, but affronted preservationists, who had managed to get the entire town listed in the National Register of Historic Places, blocked the plan. Under the banner of the Mid-Atlantic Center for the Arts (MAC), they raised enough federal and state grants for the city to buy the derelict for $90,000 in 1970. "At first they were going to use the house for artists' studios and workshops, or a playhouse," says MAC curator Diane Kerluik. "But when people heard that the Physick House was going to be saved, those who had gotten hold of pieces of the Physicks' furniture began to return it." So the relic was turned into a "museum of Victoriana" instead.

In the 1980s, thanks to $1 million in donations and additional grants—and thousands of hours of volunteer labor, workers refinished woodwork, replaced garish modern wallpaper with period paper, and purchased carpets and drapes. Fittingly, the very first restoration dollars had come from a Halloween party at Emlen Physick's old, haunted house.

*The Stick Style house that
Frank Furness built for his friend
Emlen Physick is a curious
jumble of clapboard walls,
crossing grids, dormers, and
corbeled "smokestack" chimneys.*

Children never lived in the
Physick House, but curators have
converted the cook's bedroom
into a Victorian playland.

Top: It was Victorian custom for the women of a household to devote up to two weeks to sewing each spring— sometimes with the help of $1-a-day seamstresses.

Above: While he enjoyed the company of his aunt and domineering mother who lived with him, bachelor Emlen Physick sometimes sought solitude and fresh air in his billiard room.

Overleaf: The informal family parlor includes an unusual piece of 19th-century furniture—a couch that folds backward into a double bed.

Saint Peter's Episcopal Church

Morristown, New Jersey

McKim, Mead, and White of New York designed Saint Peter's Church, with its Norman tower, in 1886. The prudent Episcopalians built nothing until they could afford it, so the church was not completed for 24 years. Opposite: The pastor can see his flock, and they him, again in the bright, refurbished sanctuary. Architect Kurt Landberg devoted even more effort to improving the acoustics.

Any late-20th-century parishioner was sure to be inspired by the 1889 Saint Peter's Church, with its imposing Norman bell tower, medieval candelabra chandeliers, soaring limestone arches, baroque high altar, and daedal stained-glass windows. How could one not sing praises to the Lord? That is, if one could see these details or hear anyone but oneself singing.

For by 1987, venerable Saint Peter's, its ceiling painted brown, and the light from clerestory windows and dim bulbs straining against the gloom, was so murky that the new rector, David P. Hegg II, could not spy his flock in the back pews, and all but the sharpest-eyed worshippers—enveloped as they were by brick walls so porous that you could blow your breath into them—could only guess at the notes in the hymnal. So dead was the sanctuary that a monogrammed shell—iconoclastically dubbed by some "Mary on the half-shell"—was needed behind the pulpit to amplify the homilist's words. Remembers the Reverend Hegg, "On a gray Sunday morning, I certainly had to kick myself into high gear to wake the congregation up."

Of course, some old-guard parishioners in fastidious, moneyed Morristown, a New York City suburb where Anglicans had held prayer book services since the early 1700s, liked the somber surroundings—and what they could see of church treasures, such as the wrought-iron rood screen across the chancel and the 1890 Louis C. Tiffany stained-glass window—just fine. Saint Peter's had, after all, been planned as a substantial sanctum by monumental New York architect Charles McKim, who would go on to restore the White House.

Would that all of the congregation could appreciate these details, worried the Reverend Hegg. "The mood was almost depressing, though those who had been here for a long time didn't realize it." With more than a subtle nudge toward change from him and building committee chairman Clarence Eich, the church approved an ambitious $2 million capital campaign. The congregation engaged prominent Episcopal Church architect Kurt Landberg of Saint Louis, and restoration began. Grimy walls were cleaned, joints caulked, ceiling panels sealed and painted a lighter hue, and windows cleaned to a fare-thee-well. The porous walls were covered with two coats of a transparent sealant, increasing fourfold the sound "reverberation time" from the pulpit.

In a much earlier capital campaign, in 1886, Saint Peter's senior warden Alfred Mills had addressed the congregation: "Thorough work is expensive, always," he said. "A good building is a necessary expense." Once they could actually see their glorious surroundings and hear each other sing, new—and most old—Saint Peter's members a century later could see his point.

San José de Gracia Church

Las Trampas, New Mexico

When Americans discuss their regional subcultures, they often overlook the Spanish culture of New Mexico's high mountains. Yet this colonial civilization led north from Mexico by priests was thriving even as Ben Franklin was flying a kite in a thunderstorm.

Among the villages 8,000 feet up in the Sangre de Cristo Mountains was the farming community of Las Trampas—"The Traps" in English—first cleared from the juniper and piñon forest by 12 families in 1751. Origin of the village's name is obscure. Beaver trapping was not introduced until the 19th century; the "traps" reference may tie to the settlers' mission, for even though they were simple bean and corn farmers, they were asked to set up a barrier against marauding Comanches. About 1761 they began building a modest chapel, the church of San José de Gracia, on the Las Trampas plaza. The church's adobe walls and crude wood roof covered with mud are Pueblo Indian in influence, but the floor plan, with a nave, apse, choir balcony, and even side chapels squeezed into the tiny sanctuary, is clearly Spanish.

Spanish is the working language at Las Trampas, and residents have rejected many chances to integrate into the larger, English-speaking society and bitterly opposed efforts to make San José de Gracia a historic site—and thus, an Anglo tourist attraction.

Today, the humble church is filled with beautiful icons and paintings, including one of a martyred Franciscan friar. Heat is still supplied by wood-burning stoves. The defensive wall and all the Spanish colonial buildings around the old plaza have disappeared. Had not villagers and volunteers periodically stepped forward to save the chapel, it too would have deteriorated and caved in from the microscopic undulation of its walls caused by the high mountains' climatic extremes. At least twice in the 20th century, help came from nationally prominent architects: John Gaw Meem, a leader of a society that preserved New Mexican mission churches, in the 1930s, and, in the 1960s, Nathaniel Owings, founding partner of Skidmore, Owings, and Merrill, who had moved to New Mexico and fallen in love with the high valleys.

By 1986 San José de Gracia's adobe walls and roof had again cracked and were beginning to crumble. With help from volunteers recruited from newspaper and television appeals, parishioners did the work themselves, making new adobe mud, repainting interior walls, cleaning icons and artwork, and scrubbing the floors. It helped that 1986 was a local election year: Candidates dropped by and left contributions. Once again, good fortune had arrived in time to save this tiny remnant of an often-overlooked American culture.

The humble mission church of Las Trampas—which residents first paid for with the fruits of their crops and livestock in 1776—is remarkably ornate inside.

Overleaf: Spanish fortifications and other plaza buildings crumbled long ago, and so, too, would have San José de Gracia had Trampaseños and Anglo friends such as Nathaniel Owings not stepped in.

Carousels

Broome County, New York

Frenchmen of the 17th century played a game called *carrousel,* in which riders on horseback speared wooden rings with lances. Early American kids rode "whirligigs"—wooden horses suspended from a revolving wheel. In 1866 Philadelphia cabinetmaker Gustav Denzel placed the horses on a rotating platform, turned by mules that plodded around a center pole.

But the carousel, that slowly spinning Xanadu of lights and wooden steeds, came only after Scottish immigrant Allan Hershell began to manufacture steam-powered "galleries" in North Tonawanda, New York. By 1891 he was shipping one a day to carnivals and beach resorts as far away as Tahiti, where the steam was produced by burning coconuts. Of the thousands of hand-carved, wooden Herschell carousels, only 19 are known to survive. Six can be found, still running every summer day, in the Triple Cities of Binghamton, Johnson City, and Endicott in central New York, where they have become the very symbol of Broome County. You can't go far without spotting a painted wooden street horse, horsey logo, or carousel slogan.

Every Broome County "merry-go-round" was donated by George F. Johnson or his heirs. Johnson, who ran the huge Endicott Johnson Shoe Company, provided his "working partner" employees with exceptional benefits, including recreation parks that had Herschell carousels. All had to have 100 percent "jumpers"—gliding up and down on poles—he directed, so no child would be consigned to a static chariot or bolted-down nag. And Johnson and his daughter, Lillian Sweet, decreed that rides always be free.

Summers of hard use, harder winters, and accumulations of paint exacted a heavy toll on the horses and other wooden animals. Some were rotted or had broken ears and tails, peeling paint, and loosened joints. And by 1989 the two carousels with Wurlitzer Military Band organs had stopped playing. So, utilizing donations and grants, the municipalities disassembled them all and sent them to R&F Design Company in Bristol, Connecticut, for complete restoration. The 60-horse carousel at Recreation Park in Binghamton was in particularly bad shape, since park employees in the 1970s had dip-stripped its horses in caustic paint remover that continued to seep into the wood long after they had been repainted. E. F. Johnson had paid $25,000 for that merry-go-round in 1925; it cost the city of Binghamton more than $140,000 to restore it.

Broome County's carousels have become a tourist attraction, but they are, foremost, a family fixture, as grandchildren of the youngsters who took the first rides and then paraded to George Johnson's office to thank him, line up for a turn in the very same saddles.

Every Broome County carousel horse is a "jumper." The "romance side" of each horse— that side facing the crowd— is more elaborate than the side facing the carousel interior. In addition, figures on the outer ring are more lavishly decorated with extra glass jewels and carved ribbons.

Main Building

Ellis Island, New York

The ornate processing center on Ellis Island, that Golden Door to a new life for 17 million immigrants to America, slammed shut in 1954. It had effectively stopped handling immigrants in the 1930s, as immigration quotas and the Depression obviated the need for the great turreted, red-brick and white-limestone Beaux Arts building. It muddled along as a Coast Guard station, World War II detention center for enemy-nation aliens, and a public health service office before the federal government abandoned it to the salt air, sea gulls, and vandals.

What architect John Belle—himself an immigrant from Wales—found when he walked the corridors on a cold winter day in 1981 were hillocks of fallen plaster, piles of snow that had blown in broken windows, and a warren of government cubicles, still eerily arrayed with desks and old typewriters, as if the staff had gone home and never come back. Years of freezing, thawing, and damp salty winds off New York Harbor had corroded the building's steel and blanched its wood. And the great symbol of Ellis Island—the staircase from the first-floor baggage room to the second-level registry hall (nicknamed the "40-second Medical" because a doctor was watching at the top to see if immigrants stumbled or lost their breath)—was completely gone.

Belle's firm of Beyer Blinder Belle would soon begin an eight-year restoration of Ellis's Main Building, privately funded by the Statue of Liberty-Ellis Island Foundation. At $315 million, the joint project would become the most ambitious in American history.

Restorers would ascend scaffolding to test the adhesion of the 28,000 tiles—laid by the Guastivino brothers of Spain in 1900—and find that only 17 required replacing. All, however, needed a cleaning to wash away 85 years of grime and restore their almost mother-of-pearl luminescence. Belle and his crews turned the old baggage room into an orientation center with displays of trunks and suitcases. Other artifacts like passports, reading-test cards, and a picture puzzle—used to determine the mental acuity of the immigrants—were donated during the restoration. Oral histories were also collected for exhibit in the old office space.

"It's a sad commentary on national priorities," says John Belle, "that Ellis sat there for more than 25 years without any public commitment of funds, that the restoration stopped with the Main Building, and that money could not be found to restore the other buildings on the island. One great bureaucracy built and ran Ellis Island, and then another bureaucracy let it go to hell." But public pressure, and public generosity, can also stir bureaucracies into action, as Belle and the Statue of Liberty-Ellis Island Foundation proved on the "Isle of Tears."

*Ellis Island's processing center
replaced a wood structure
destroyed by fire in 1897. A
little-known New York firm,
Boring and Tilton, won the
design contract for a new,
fireproof center.*

Biltmore House

Asheville, North Carolina

Opposite: Biltmore conservators have been gingerly removing and restoring, one at a time, tapestries such as the 16th-century Flemish Vulcan and Venus creations in the banquet hall. Overleaf: Biltmore curators located the French company that created the original, deteriorating, silk and velvet coverings in Edith Vanderbilt's Louis XV–style bedroom—and commissioned exact copies.

Not even a multimillionaire would attempt a wholesale restoration of the four-acre, 225-room Biltmore House, the largest private home in America, built by art collector and world traveler George W. Vanderbilt in 1895. Instead, the staff has singled out limited projects each year. One emphasis was on nine of the estate's 16th-century Flemish tapestries. Vanderbilt had criss-crossed Europe to find, among others, treasures from the Flemish *Triumph of the Seven Virtues* series. Tapestries often were made in sets of five to 10, and the Biltmore owns, from the *Virtues* series, the only known "Prudence" left in the world. In 1988 the Biltmore hired a textile conservator, Patricia Ewer of New York, to work on one tapestry at a time.

In the 1950s the estate first opened to the public the Louis XV– style bedroom of Vanderbilt's wife, Edith, which had been decorated with gold silk wall and bed coverings, trimmed in purple. The fabric deteriorated, and in the 1980s, Biltmore curatorial researchers identified the company that created the original fabric— Tassinari & Chatel of Lyon, France. Using the same looms and jacquard cards as they did 100 years earlier, the French weavers took more than three years to re-create the silk, cut velvet, yellow satin, and trims.

One of the most intricate restorations involved the library's paneled ceiling, which a conservation team from England carefully removed, cleaned, and reinstalled. And to accommodate the curiosity of guests who wonder about off-limits "back of the house" restoration, the staff began behind-the-scenes tours of rooms such as Mrs. Vanderbilt's maid's quarters, a sewing room, and even a sub-basement with its boiler room and marble-backed electric breaker.

Almost since George Washington Vanderbilt began the purchase of 125,000 acres of farms, woods, and forested hillsides, historic preservation of the Biltmore Estate and Frederick Law Olmsted gardens has been, not a project, but a never-ending process.

Work continues on the Biltmore House around 1900. Construction sheds are still visible in front and gardens have not yet been fully planted. (Biltmore Estate)

Cornelia Vanderbilt, left, with her mother, Edith, c. 1905. George Vanderbilt met Edith Stuyvesant Dresser in Europe and married her in Paris in 1898. Cornelia was their only child. (Biltmore Estate)

A baleful beast guards the main
entrance to Biltmore, designed
by Vanderbilt's friend, Richard
Hunt, who was strongly
influenced by the châteaus
of the French Renaissance.

This throne, as well as an
elaborate carved mural above
the fireplace in the banquet
hall, are the work of American
sculptor Karl Bitter.

Old Salem

Winston-Salem, North Carolina

Two tides of "historic" rejuvenation rolled across America in the 1980s, picking up converts like pebbles in the surf. One was the "quick and dirty" approach, in which old places were given a coat of colonially correct paint and stuffed with period artifacts. The other was "adaptive use," in which old structures were turned into bed and breakfasts and the like.

The Moravian village of Old Salem, a block from downtown Winston-Salem, rode neither wave. Old Salem, Inc.—the nonprofit organization that had nurtured the historic 19th-century village since 1950—instead hied to a standard of authentic, even academic, restoration. Old Salem richly tells its history as a Moravian missionary outpost, while carefully preserving its alter ego as a rowdy frontier supply post. Old Salem's inventory of fine barrels, kitchenware, woodwork, and handwoven clothes is testament to its mercantile past.

In the 1980s Old Salem, Inc., launched its own archeology program. Researchers discovered, for instance, that one house was ostentatiously ornamental, its trim executed in green and a mustardy, almost "dayglow" orange—and restored it accordingly. "The people who came out of the 1950s, 1960s, and 1970s with concepts of Colonial Revival—the pastel colors—were appalled, shocked," says John Larsen, Old Salem's vice president of restoration. In another house, Old Salem, Inc., removed furnishings that did not correctly match the 1840 interpretation date—to the point that some people now walk through and wonder where all the furniture is. Out, too, during landscape restoration, went golf-course-quality greens, and in went horticultural "vignettes"—stone yards, cultivated terraced gardens, and rows of fruit bushes and trees. Beehives are tended, compost piles maintained, and rye and tobacco are harvested.

There is also increasing dialogue about *social* history, including an extensive African American interpretation program that examines the role of the many blacks who were initially welcomed into Salem but later isolated as the broader culture of the American South took hold.

Despite its insistence upon academic historic restoration, Old Salem has generated about $40 million, directly and indirectly, in annual tourism revenues. That's a business perspective quite fitting for a town where hard-headed Moravian merchants once flourished.

Landscaping is central to the restoration of Old Salem, where gardens were an extension of the household. Even the cemetery, "God's Acre," has received almost academically thorough attention.

Moravian settlers Charlotte and Timothy Vogler catch a breeze, c. 1895. Vogler, a gunsmith for more than 50 years, ran the debt-ridden Salem Tavern for a time. (Old Salem, Inc.)

Devils Lake Rehabilitations

Devils Lake, North Dakota

For years windswept North Dakota has been losing farms to consolidation. Young people have left the state, leaving behind older relatives who have looked to regional centers like Williston and Jamestown and Devils Lake for safe, clean, and affordable housing. But these towns, with their modest core of public and commercial buildings, had few apartment buildings ready-made for conversion to senior-citizen or low-cost housing.

One person who addressed this need was Devils Lake native Gary L. Stenson. A housing specialist for U.S. Senator Walter Mondale, he returned to the Minneapolis area to practice law and then to establish a company in Saint Paul, MetroPlains Development, which dug back into Stenson's rural roots to turn historic, usually vacant, buildings into affordable housing, often for senior citizens. In each venture, Stenson or MetroPlains was general partner, while local limited partners provided most of the financing. At Devils Lake, a town of 7,500 on North Dakota's "drift plains" and once home to picturesque chautauqua grounds, MetroPlains developed five projects: 1. The 1911 Great Northern Hotel, once a first-class railroad hotel popular with hunters and boaters, as a home for the elderly. "We bought it from the county after it had been turned back for nonpayment of taxes," says Stenson. 2. The 1912 Fire Station No. 1, declared surplus property when the city built a new station. It was rehabilitated into nine low- and moderate-income units. 3. The 1936 Gilbertson Funeral Home, which MetroPlains turned into 31 units. 4. The 1895 Wineman Opera House block. In 1907, Morris Glickson opened a clothing store that remains in business in the building, beneath Stenson's restored apartment units. 5. The 1909 neoclassical Saint Mary's Academy Catholic school. The academy had been abandoned for four years following a devastating fire when Stenson got involved in restoring it, for $1.2 million, as the renamed Academy Park; this was not a low-income project. Academy Park is now a prestige Devils Lake address.

Stenson estimates that the development cost per apartment unit among the five projects is $40,000. MetroPlains has utilized two relatively little-known affordable-housing programs to help finance many of its restorations: the Internal Revenue Service's Low Income Housing Tax Credit plan and a Farmers Home Administration program. The latter has seen more than 415,000 units constructed throughout the Farm Belt, serving 830,000 elderly and low-income persons—with fewer than one percent defaults. One of the out-of-the-limelight communities where these programs have put on a human face is Devils Lake, North Dakota.

Horse-drawn wagons were still in vogue in the early 1920s, a decade after Fire Hall No. 1 was built. It is now low- and moderate-income housing. (State Historical Society of North Dakota) Opposite: Restored by Gary Stenson as housing for the elderly and handicapped, the Great Northern Hotel was once a first-class railroad hotel— a favorite haunt of hunters and boaters.

232

Over-the-Rhine

Cincinnati, Ohio

If the world ended, Mark Twain is said to have declared with a wink, he wanted to be in Cincinnati, because there "it wouldn't happen for ten more years."

Cincinnati's methodical ways were good for its historic Over-the-Rhine District. By the time the Queen City got geared up for urban renewal, the federal government was out of the business, and 1,500 or so old buildings had escaped demolition.

In the 1860s and 1870s, German immigrants had poured into Cincinnati, constructing *biergartens*, breweries, churches, and brick apartment buildings along the old Miami and Erie Canal that reached to the Great Lakes. The canal became "the Rhine," and the sprawling, 362-acre tenement district alongside it, "Over-the-Rhine," which an 1886 publication promoting immigration to Cincinnati called "more German than Germany itself."

With 300,000 residents hemmed in by steep hillsides and the canal, Over-the-Rhine at the turn of the century ranked as the densest place in America, more crowded than Brooklyn or South Philadelphia. Most of its three- and four-story brick structures—with their distinctive lintels, frieze windows, and "two-over-two-light" window sashes—were poorly ventilated warrens of apartments that looked down on streets jammed with people and slaughterhouse-bound pigs ("Pigopolis" was the area's unflattering nickname).

But Over-the-Rhine's cachet faded in the 1930s as second-generation Germans left to build single-family homes "in the heights." An underclass of Irish immigrants, black migrants, and Appalachian whites streamed in, occupying run-down buildings no one else wanted. By the 1950s, Over-the-Rhine had slid into the slough of poverty, homelessness, crime, and decay.

In the 1980s Greater Cincinnati rediscovered Over-the-Rhine, setting off a battle of wills. Drawn by the neighborhood's historic character and proximity to downtown, investors began buying and refurbishing buildings along Main Street; near the Findlay open-air market; and around Washington Park, where the original Germans once staged vigorous musical and gymnastic events. But gentrification was opposed by advocates for low-income residents, who saw the basin as their last bastion of decent housing. Because of the enduring distrust, a master plan hammered out in 1984–85 contained no implementation strategy, so controls on development could not be put in place. As a result, renovated buildings offering pricey loft apartments rub elbows with worn-out rattraps. City planners concede that an upscaling of Over-the-Rhine will come side-by-side with affordable housing, or not at all, and that, say those who see promise in both its oompah-German and its proud-ghetto traditions, is as it should be.

Over-the-Rhine restorers respected the historic character of the district's buildings, retaining the distinctive window moldings, the two-over-two sash, ground-floor storefronts, and stylish cornice treatments. Here, the porcine streetgoers, however, are a modern addition.

The Powerhouse

Cleveland, Ohio

If you lived on the west side of Cleveland in 1920, and took the streetcar downtown, you crossed the long Detroit-Superior Bridge over an industrial basin called "the Flats," and acrid smoke from steel mills, breweries, and manufacturing plants below curled around you.

Two of the belching smokestacks belonged to the Powerhouse, the 100,000-square-foot coal-burning plant that industrialist Marcus Hanna built in 1892 to run his Woodland & West Side Street Railway. John N. Richardson, a Scottish-born Cleveland architect, created the red-brick Romanesque Revival building, which featured arched windows, a 200-foot smokestack, clerestories, and Dutch gables. A new wing in 1901 added a second, 226-foot chimney.

By 1925 automobiles were puttering over the Detroit-Superior Bridge, and Hanna's streetcar line had been absorbed by another company that had its own source of electricity. The Powerhouse was simply abandoned. It sat mostly empty as sooty old factories around it closed and moved, and buildings were left to the vagaries of decay. Only taverns and flophouses held on.

In 1974 an engineering firm purchased the Powerhouse and announced it would begin a $5 million Cannery Row–type facelift. But just after its crews had torn off the roof, financing collapsed. The renovation was scrubbed, and for another decade the industrial dinosaur would sit topless and empty—save for 30-foot trees that sprouted from the basement muck.

In the 1980s, Cleveland's Jacobs Investments Inc. began turning much of the Flats into an ambitious "festival marketplace" of riverfront cafés, retail shops, and night spots. In 1988 the company launched a $15 million redevelopment of the old Powerhouse, which it had bought three years earlier for $450,000. Because the Powerhouse was a National Register property, architect Robert Corna could not dismantle the facade or mangle the interior walls. In effect, he had to raise a building within a building by erecting a new supporting structure, metal-plate stairs, and raw-pine floors. As crews were disassembling the exterior bricks (whose mortar had turned to sand) on the 1892 section, a howling blizzard toppled a giant crane, knocking out the south wall. The old section was rebuilt using original bricks. Cleveland architecture critic Carol Poh Miller called the finished building, which has drawn more than a million patrons a year since its opening in 1989, an architectural triumph and a "preservation success story." But she panned the tenant mix as "Disneyland on the Cuyahoga" and the sanitized Flats around the Powerhouse as "sterile."

One irony did not escape other trained eyes: The power plant that had once generated enough electricity to run a city streetcar system was now heated and cooled by natural gas.

The truss system in the atrium is original to the old Powerhouse. Since the building had sat open for years, the trusses were rusted, but they were removed, cleaned, reinforced, and returned.

Overleaf: Today the view of the Powerhouse in the Flats is spectacular. But it was not long ago that ochre soot obscured the skyline and the Cuyahoga River was a rainbow of chemical colors.

Round Barn

Arcadia, Oklahoma

Opposite: Both Big Bill Odor and the 1980s restoration team used the same technique to bend the Round Barn's burr-oak timbers. They soaked them for weeks.

Overleaf: After Luke Robison and his men succeeded in "unscrewing" the twisted and roofless barn, they were able to save 70 percent of its boards in restoring its walls and roof.

While rectangular barns across America touted Mail Pouch tobacco, Odor grabbed a buck from an Oklahoma City department store in 1909. (Arcadia Historical and Preservation Society)

A s a farmer living in the heart of America's Tornado Alley, "Big Bill" Odor knew a thing or two about whirlwinds and eggs. Folks hereabouts think they were the factors that sealed his decision to build a round barn when he got his own 320-acre place in Arcadia in 1898. No doubt he had seen twisters make toothpicks of rectangular barns, and he figured a round one with an egg-shaped roof, tiny windows, and small doors would stand a better chance in a tornado.

His logic—or luck—held. His 43-foot-tall, 60-feet-diameter barn—made with fresh-cut burr oak that Odor soaked in the Deep Fork River and bent in rounded molds he had crafted—stood for 90 years. It might have held up even longer had not a later owner, Frank Vrana, enlarged the downstairs door and failed to brace it. Thereafter, ever so slowly, the barn started to twist and slump to the east, and then the roof finally fell in.

The unornamented barn was the town's favorite dance spot, a popular photo stop for passersby on scenic, two-lane U.S. 66, and a sure-fire subject for artists. After Frank Vrana died in 1974, the barn stood empty and contorting until the mid-1980s, when his six daughters decided to donate it to someone who might preserve it. First to express interest was the Historic Preservation Trust in nearby Edmond, which went so far as to get officials talking about annexing Arcadia. That got Arcadia's attention! While the town's own preservation society raised funds, Luke Robison, a retired contractor who loved a challenge, set up some scaffolding at the barn, intending to fix the roof. Fortunately, he was away when it caved in with a "whoosh" after a violent thunderstorm.

Undaunted, Robison and others wrapped guy wires around the barn, attached them to turnbuckles and borrowed utility poles, and tightened the buckles until the crooked building was "unscrewed." Where replacements were needed, Robison's men soaked and bent burr-oak boards, à la Big Bill Odor. They repaired the foundation, put on a new roof, then painted the barn red, because red was the color everyone remembered from its Route 66 heyday. The whole restoration cost Arcadia's historical society just $60,000—one-fifth the Edmond group's estimate and much of it covered by appreciative visitors' donations.

"If the Jobes really had come by headin' for California in *The Grapes of Wrath*, they'd have seen the round barn," says Luke Robison. "Sixty-some years later, she's still here."

Pendleton Depot

Pendleton, Oregon

Almost there. The trappers' settlement that would become Pendleton was, in the 1840s and 1850s, almost the end of the Oregon Trail. But first the dauntless settlers on the Great Migration faced one last, treacherous trek through the Blue Mountains before the first snow. Then it was, literally, all downhill to the splendor of the lush Willamette Valley. Anxious to press on, these voyagers did not tarry long, and it was only with homesteading in the 1860s that a town rose along the sparkling Umatilla River; it was incorporated in 1880 and named after U.S. Senator George Hunt Pendleton of Ohio, whom some of the townspeople knew. A year later the railroad reached town, linking it to Omaha's stockyards and Portland's mills.

In 1910 the Union Pacific Railroad replaced an old wood-chalet depot with a mission-style red-brick station. It was the vernacular depot of the day, with a red-pipe roof, wide overhang supported by wooden brackets, and a trackside operator's bay. In it, a telegrapher would send and accept messages, affix notes to a shepherd's crook, and stretch them up to passing engineers. By the 1920s the Pendleton Round-Up rodeo was already a tourist attraction, and, come early September, "Girl Greeters" in western outfits met each train. Year-round, boys hired by the depot newsstand would walk the platform, peddling fruit and Cracker Jacks.

By 1971 the Union Pacific had ended passenger service to Pendleton and moved most of its freight operations out of town. It kept the depot as offices, but by 1984 it had no further use for the station and planned to tear it down. The city, though, had already identified the depot as a historic resource that must be preserved. The railroad fought the ordinance, then relented, agreeing to lease the depot to the city for $1 a year. The Umatilla County Historical Society, which had eyed the depot for use as a museum, signed a contract (recouping the city its $1 a year), assumed insurance liability, and began restoration. "The pipes had burst," says society board member Rudy Rada. "There was no furniture. A lot of plaster had fallen. It was a mess." Thanks to grants, $45,000 in cash saved for just such a move, and countless volunteer hours by artisans, the society restored and furnished the old depot in time for a grand opening in 1988.

Unlike the Pendleton Underground attraction, whose actors spice up the story of the city's bordellos, gaming halls, and opium dens, the museum plays history straight. All but a few railroad artifacts disappeared with the ebbing of service. So the depot mounts displays about farms, Indian culture, and Pendleton's famous mills as it greets travelers crossing the Blue Mountains on the modern-day, interstate-highway version of the Oregon Trail.

Below: Where Amtrak trains make their infrequent stops today, "silkworm specials" once raced by. Tracks were cleared for trains hurrying the perishable Chinese worms east.

Bottom: The wires to La Grande to the southeast and Spokane to the north no longer "sing," but this telegrapher's set—a highlight of the depot museum—still works.

Timberline Lodge

Mount Hood, Oregon

These were no slouching leaf-rakers, the 150 or so Works Progress Administration hirelings who rode the first canvas-flap trucks up a crude dirt road just cleared of snow to report for work at the timberline, 6,000 feet up the southern face of Mount Hood. Here, unskilled laborers and expert masons, muscular blacksmiths, and carpenters adept in the use of the broadax and adze would build a gargantuan mountain lodge—a majestic monument to human creativity and craftsmanship at the height of personal desperation.

In Portland 55 miles away, 100 other workers—many of them women on relief—hooked the lodge's rugs from rags and old Civilian Conservation Corps uniforms and blankets, sewed appliquéd curtains, and hammered ashtrays out of copper and andirons out of railroad ties. They painted canvases and fashioned 820 pieces of "Cascadian" furniture and decorations, including newel posts in the shape of mountain animals and Indian-theme carvings whose designs were copied from Campfire Girl manuals.

Designed by the U.S. Forest Service regional engineers' office, the immense, chalet-style Timberline Lodge rose midway up the south side of Wy'East, as the Indians called Oregon's highest mountain (11,235 feet). Dormered wings veered from the hexagonal core, or head house, with its 400-ton, 92-foot central chimney and 750-pound weather vane. Workers cried openly at the lodge's formal dedication in 1937, not at President Franklin Roosevelt's words of thanks, but at having to leave a project that had given them months of bread and dignity.

By the late 1970s, millions of guests in snow-packed boots had stomped through Timberline Lodge, turning rugs threadbare, fraying upholstery, and wearing down woodwork. Since the 1980s, carpenters, seamstresses, stonemasons, weavers, rug hookers, and landscapers, directed by the nonprofit Friends of Timberline, went to work restoring fabrics and rugs; rewebbing and making new furniture from WPA blueprints; conserving watercolors and lithographs inside; and beautifying outside. Key to the $2 million restoration was the addition of a day lodge for skiers, taking punishing traffic away from the 1937 building. Ironically, the work could backfire— if Timberline Lodge once again becomes too popular.

En route to Bonneville Dam in 1937, President Roosevelt did double dedication duty at Timberline Lodge. It meant the end to lifesaving paychecks for construction workers. (Friends of Timberline)

Opposite: Furnishings, created as a make-work project in Portland, melded pioneer and Indian motifs. Because beams were hand cut on site from green wood, they cracked extensively as they dried over the years.

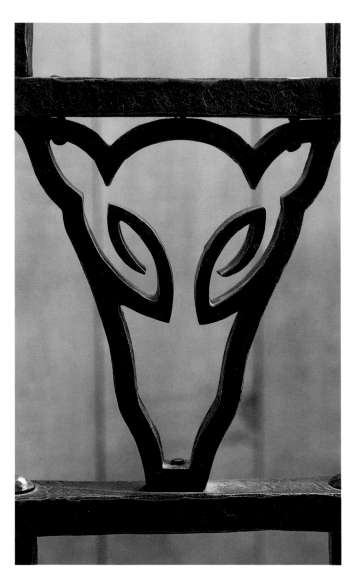

Orion B. Dawson fashioned this
Cascade Dining Room gate, one
of more than 1,500 pieces of
structural and ornamental
ironwork—including andirons
forged from railroad rails.

Rustic newel posts were hewn
from discarded cedar telephone
poles into the shape of forest
animals. Thousands of hands
getting a grip while rounding
corners have given the posts a
natural sheen.

WPA worker Tom Lamon
executed this "optifectal
[opaque] glass" mosaic, "Bring
on the Mountain," just inside
the main lodge door. He used
leftover glass from a bigger
"Babe the Blue Ox" glass mural.

Hotel Atop the Bellevue

Philadelphia, Pennsylvania

From the moment Prussian immigrant George Boldt opened the $8 million, 1,094-room Bellevue Stratford Hotel in 1904 with the grandest party in city history, his creation was the center of social and political life in Philadelphia. All the leading clubs that did not own their own buildings met at the enormous French Renaissance–style hotel. Philosophically, a stay at the Bellevue Stratford was deliberately modeled after a pampered ocean-liner journey.

But by the middle of the century, the hotel concluded that elegance was out, sleek was in. Trumpeting the slogan, "Old in Grace, New in Face," the Bellevue Stratford hid its great columned portico behind glass and aluminum, obscured the lobby's soaring coffers under a drop ceiling, and replaced overstuffed and inlaid furniture with blond, laminated pieces. Occupancy slid, and whispers about closing the hotel turned to roars when a hotelier's nightmare struck.

Within a month of getting home from a week of U.S. Bicentennial festivities in 1976, 182 American Legion members became violently ill; 29 died. All had stayed at the Bellevue Stratford Hotel. While it would be shown that this "Legionnaires' Disease," contracted from bacteria in the mists of cooling units, drinking fountains, and shower heads, had shown up in isolated cases at old hotels worldwide, its concentration at the Bellevue Stratford drove the hotel over the edge. After limping along nearly empty, losing $10,000 a day, the owner, Banker's Securities Corporation, closed the hotel on November 18, 1976.

Seven months later, Rubin Associates, a developer of shopping centers and office buildings, bought the hotel for $8.25 million—about what it had cost to build in 1904— and embarked upon a $25 million rehabilitation directed by Hyman Myers. On September 26, 1979, the hotel, again elegant, reopened as the Fairmont, managed by the chain of the same name. But occupancy was weak. An aggressive chain, Westin Hotels, took over and restored the name "Bellevue Stratford." Westin wooed back social clubs and party planners, but it missed an important point: There simply were not enough high-end travelers to Philadelphia to fill the several new luxury hotels. Citing mounting financial losses, Westin closed the Bellevue Stratford in March 1986.

Rubin Associates reassessed and determined to reopen the building as a retail and office center topped by a smaller, 170-room hotel, the Hotel Atop the Bellevue. This second rehabilitation, also designed by Hyman Myers, cost four times as much as the first. Myers tore out the middle wing of the old E-shaped hotel and created an atrium, topped by the historic Rose Garden. The Bellevue's famous library, Founders restaurant, and Ethel Barrymore Lounge were meticulously restored.

There's an irony at work at the Hotel Atop the Bellevue, harking back to the Bellevue Stratford's days of ocean-liner attentiveness: Its management firm is the Cunard Company.

The palatial 1904 French Renaissance–style Bellevue Stratford had an undulating terra-cotta facade, capped by a slate mansard roof with corner towers crowned by ornate iron spires. (Davidson Bros.)

Windows in the Ethel Barrymore reception room—obscured behind drywall in a desperate "Old in Face, New in Grace" renovation in the 1960s—again offer sweeping views of the skyline.

The Priory

Pittsburgh, Pennsylvania

History lovers Ed and Mary Ann Graf bought a double local landmark in 1984 after Ed's advertising agency had passed on the property: the 1852 Saint Mary's German Catholic Church and its adjacent 1888 home for Benedictine priests and brothers in the historic Deutschtown section. The Italianate church, with its Byzantine domes and priory, afforded a view of Pittsburgh's burgeoning Golden Triangle, but unfortunately an even cozier look at the city's latest freeway. The price was right—$106,000—because of the freeway. It had displaced the largely German parish, which merged with Italian and Polish ones nearby.

The priory was what a later guest called "sort of a holy dormitory" for priests and brothers of the 1,500-year-old monastic order—and a way station for travelers to the Benedictines' Saint Vincent Archabbey in Latrobe, Pennsylvania. In 1986, the Grafs, after obtaining the necessary $1 million from loans, grants from preservation organizations, and their own savings, rehabilitated the parish house into a 24-room, European-style hotel called "The Priory—a City Inn." They had expanded their original idea of a simple bed-and-breakfast after friends pointed out that the North Side neighborhood, home to two hospitals and several corporate headquarters, lacked an appropriate hotel. Ironically, the elevated freeway sealed the decision, since it dropped an exit (and potential customers) only a few blocks away.

The restoration challenge, according to Mary Ann Graf, long a board member of the Pittsburgh Historical Landmarks Foundation, "was like seeing a decrepit, badly dressed old lady fall in the street, and you go pick her up, brush her off, and restore her dignity." Among other things, crews replaced flooring damaged by water; preserved the 14-foot-high stamped-metal ceilings; and used a hydraulic lift to hoist 20 armoires—which could not be maneuvered around sharp turns in the grand staircase—through second- and third-story windows. The result is an intimate hotel whose courtyard backdrop is the backlighted Saint Mary's Church. This is next on the Grafs' agenda; they foresee it as a facility for parties and small trade shows.

The perspective out the front door, toward the expressway, is less serene. A brothel once flourished where a high-rise senior citizen center now partially obscures the Pittsburgh skyline, and Benedictines who still stop by to bring *benediktusbröt*—monks' bread—from Latrobe say that when the bishop found out about its activities, he closed the curtains and moved priests to the back rooms. Now in the front parlor where priests perhaps sneaked peeks around the shades, Victorian-style weddings are enthusiastically performed at the Priory city inn.

Spared from its scheduled demolition to make room for a freeway, the Benedictine priory was converted into a "city inn" by amateur historians and antique hounds Ed and Mary Ann Graf.

Rose Island Lighthouse

Newport, Rhode Island

O f the 900 or so light stations—lighthouses with keepers' quarters—that once ringed the coastlines and the Great Lakes of the United States, half are gone, having fallen to the ravages of storms, shelling during the nation's early wars, and the predations of vandals. Some are mere poles with radio beacons, and all but one—the Boston Light Station—are automated.

One old light station that's been turned into a museum and hostel—with an unusual environmental twist—sits on Rose Island in the east passage of lower Narragansett Bay. Narrangansett Indians, British and French soldiers, and quarantined cholera victims all lived on the island, which in the 20th century was also a torpedo station and ammunition dump.

Rose Island's lighthouse sent out its steady-red beam from 1869 until 1971, when a series of lights was incorporated into a new bridge across the bay. The early, civilian keepers of the Rose Island lighthouse were hardy and often brave men; one, Charles Curtis, who stayed with his family on the island from 1887 to 1918 maintaining the light and the compressors that sounded the island's foghorn, earned two medals for lifesaving during his tenure. The last civilian keeper left Rose Island in 1941; the lighthouse was maintained by Coast Guardsmen for the next 30 years. The lighthouse and its surrounding cliffs and sand hills changed hands several times, from 1960, when the U.S. General Services Administration sold Rose Island to the city of Newport for $2,300, until 1985, when the city turned it over to an independent, nonprofit corporation, the Rose Island Lighthouse Foundation, with a charge to renovate, operate, and maintain it at no expense to taxpayers.

Photographs provided by Paul Stedman, grandson of keeper Jesse Orton, enabled the foundation's volunteer restorers to tackle the lighthouse's deteriorated clapboard walls, slate mansard roof, and window and door trim. During its years of abandonment, vandals had stolen most of the hardware and the foghorns, torn out all the doors, and even ripped the cast-iron radiators from the floor and thrown them through upper windows to the rocks below. Using pictures sent by descendants of keepers—and $350,000 in grants, raffle proceeds, and donated labor—the foundation restored and restocked the entire house.

One driving force was environmentalist Charlotte Johnson, who has since become the foundation's executive director. At her urging, a visit to the island has become an environmental adventure. Electricity and water are strictly monitored, and composting and beach clean-up are part of the daily routine for staff and guests alike. "Why not show people how to be self-sufficient?" asks Johnson. "It's a mind-altering experience, without the drugs."

The lighthouse was a family home as well as sentinel station. Once a week, the keeper would sail to town for provisions, towing a skiff. Now the house is the center of an important environmental adventure.

Opposite: It's possible to spend the night with today's keepers at the Rose Island Lighthouse. Visitors get "environmentally conscious" instruction and can help with chores and beach clean-up.

Above: Rose Island's small light, covered in red, was one of a series (others the more familiar oscillating white) that gave mariners their bearings. Its foghorn helped, too, in foul weather.

Kensington Manor

Eastover, South Carolina

Not only was Kensington Manor—with its delicate plasterwork and ironwork— allowed to deteriorate, its farmer-owner also stored hay, vats of chemicals, and fertilizer in its rooms and hallways.

A 29-room Renaissance Revival villa on South Carolina's antebellum Kensington Plantation was so bedraggled when the Union Camp Corporation came upon it in 1981 that it was being used as a barn to store soybeans and fertilizer. A grain chute poked though a parlor window, the French skylight lay in shards, and bins of pesticides filled the dining room. Long gone to thieves were the marble mantelpieces and most of the hardware and plumbing.

The corporation's scout was there because the market for white paper had mushroomed with the growth of computer use, and Union Camp—based in Virginia and a maker of forest products, chemicals, and fragrances—was looking for a site for a new, $600 million fine-paper mill. It settled on 4,000 acres on four combined parcels south of Columbia, the South Carolina state capital. In answer to community pleas, Union Camp agreed to restore the Big House through its "land legacy program"—leaving land surrounding the mill site in cotton and soybeans, and setting aside another portion as an alligator, deer, and bird preserve. The corporation pledged to "spend what it takes" to restore Kensington Manor. "What it takes" would be $750,000.

Kensington was built in 1852–54 by Matthew Richard Singleton, a wealthy cotton planter who had the misfortune of dying before he could enjoy the house that grew in a most unusual way out of the smaller family home. The estate's 235 slaves, guided by architects, literally had cut the house in half and pushed it to each side, then built in the fabulous center core with its barrel-vaulted ceiling, high steps, and fancy wood balustrade.

Kensington Manor passed through family, friends', and the U.S. government's hands before a local family bought it following World War II. They moved into a modern brick house and turned the old manor house into a makeshift granary and shed. The South Carolina Department of Archives and History and community groups fought to preserve Kensington Manor. But they did not own it, and they had little money.

Union Camp had no such problems. Supervisor Ralph Boyd's crews stabilized the crumbling foundation, then recast and repaired plasterwork, and repainted the house—a tricky proposition, since the exterior was down to bare wood. The closest that chemical analysis could determine from a few faded fragments was that the very first color had been cream. Cream it became, with gray trim and a red replacement terneplate roof. Union Camp offers free tours that more than 30 employee docents have been trained to conduct. Had not the rise of computer use and the demand for printer paper got the faraway corporation poking around the property, there likely would have been nothing but the ruins of an old plantation house to visit.

The original manor house had no central section. Under the direction of architects, the house was cut in half, the two sections moved aside, and an elaborate center portion added.

Miles Brewton House

Charleston, South Carolina

In the inspirations of an erudite owner, an enlightened contractor, a consummate woodcarver, and a master of the art form of papier-mâché, history has repeated itself in the Miles Brewton House to restore what may be America's finest surviving Georgian town home.

In 1765–69 in what was then Charles Town, the owner was Brewton, a state assemblyman who had made his fortune in the slave trade; the contractor Richard Moncrief, the premier builder in the port's boom years before the American Revolution; and the principal craftsman of the rococo woodwork was Ezra Waite, who had left London for opportunities in the "most British" of colonial cities. The name of the man who masterfully executed delicate papier-mâché lintels, layered with gold leaf, does not survive. They had their counterparts in the late 1980s, beginning with owner Peter Manigault, chairman of the board of the *Charleston Post* and *Courier* and former vice chairman of the National Trust for Historic Preservation.

Remarkable details are everywhere in the house, which has never been sold: a delicately incised fretwork frieze; an elliptical fanlight above the front entrance; faux-mahogany wainscoting; overlapping square sheets of 18th-century wallpaper; and the distinctive papier-mâché, said to be the oldest remaining in an American private residence. Earthquakes and even vicious Hurricane Hugo in 1989 barely scathed the structure, but human activities—including the application of 16 layers of paint that clogged the intricate woodwork—took a toll.

Manigault determined to restore the house in a fashion befitting its nonpareil stature. Among the work: Contractor Tommy Graham and his artisans painstakingly "depainted" the house with heat guns and dental picks. Carver John Bivins of Wilmington, North Carolina, copied and replaced broken or missing elements in the woodwork's embellishments. And, from a single piece that a rat had once carried to her nest behind a column capital, papier-mâché man Jonathan Thornton of Buffalo, New York, was able to create one whole repeat to scale in the drawing room.

"This house has been an interesting place to study the line between utility and aesthetics," says Peter Manigault, "a place where architecture is a reflection of contemporary life. Bringing that back here has been an adventure."

A chandelier, argand lamps, and landscape painting embellish the Miles Brewton House's parlor with its magnificent rococo plasterwork and faux-mahogany doorway.

Renowned for its delicate woodwork outside as well as in, the house is a classic "double house"—a double-length ballroom wide upstairs— uncommon in Charleston.

Deadwood Historic District

Deadwood, South Dakota

The Dakotas' most notorious town was laid out along one main street in the summer of 1876, after the cry of "Gold!" had emptied other settlements and filled Deadwood Gulch with 25,000 people. But Deadwood did not wither and die like so many boom towns. The discovery of silver followed gold strikes; it became the county seat, and shrewd marketing unabashedly spread the word that Deadwood was "South Dakota's Playtown."

Exuberantly marketed were the colorful eccentrics who once strutted through Deadwood, including gunman James Butler "Wild Bill" Hickock, who died ignominiously from a Jack McCall bullet to the back of the head; "Calamity Jane" Burke, a hard-drinking harlot with a heart of gold; and Seth Bullock, whiskey purveyor, sheriff, and pal of Theodore Roosevelt, whom Bullock met during Teddy's "western period" of unabated outdoorsy male bonding. In 1895 Bullock built a three-story hotel that he named after himself.

The mines played out for good during World War II, and other South Dakota attractions like Mount Rushmore and a mega-drugstore in tiny Wall upstaged the old frontier town. In the 1980s Deadwood's elders beheld a decaying town filled with firetrap hotels, struggling summertime gift shops, and a proliferation of 1950s aluminum storefronts, phony knotty pine facades, and flickering neon signs. In 1989 the National Trust for Historic Preservation listed Deadwood among the 11 most endangered historic sites in America.

Desperate for a facelift, the town hitched its wagon to two unlikely steeds: gaming and historic restoration. Voters statewide approved the 1989 referendum permitting low-stakes gaming in Deadwood—with a percentage of the take going directly to restoration. The city spent this windfall—$20 million in the first two years alone—to restore streets and public buildings. Preservation money also was loaned to business owners for their own restorations, including the pink-and-white cut sandstone Bullock Hotel, with its trademark cornice and cupola, which had degenerated into a frumpy boarding house. Using $327,000, according to Mark Wolfe, the city's historic preservation officer, managing partner Mary Schmit saw to it that workers "took every bit of woodwork, such as mahogany pilasters, that they could possibly find and kept it, restored it, and put it back." Restored, too, was the Italianate Bodega Saloon, where a giant Coca-Cola sign on the side of a brick wall was repainted. A replica of the saloon's c. 1910 electric sign also was installed.

As awnings came down to better reveal Main Street's Victorian architecture, Deadwood found something more than a pull on a slot machine to offer visitors. "Anybody can build a fake Old West town," says Wolfe. "But Deadwood is the real thing."

No longer rip-roaring,
Deadwood has married two
unlikely forces—gaming and
historic restoration—to clean
up its act, its historic structures,
and its streets.

Willey & Williams Building

Sioux Falls, South Dakota

By 1880, nine years before Dakota Territory became two states, Governor Nehemiah Ordway desperately needed someone to come and design public buildings. A New Hampshireman by birth, he thought of architect Wallace Dow, of Croyden, New Hampshire. Dow moved west and began an illustrious career designing civic buildings—most in red Sioux quartzite.

On Main Avenue in his adopted hometown, which was thriving as a milling and meatpacking center, Dow designed the gigantic, Richardsonian Romanesque Minnehaha County Courthouse. In its shadow, catty-corner across the street in 1891, he drew a three-story office and residential building for the owners of the booming Merchants' Hotel to accommodate spillover guests. The first floor was rented out as wholesale space.

With its limestone trim, bay windows on the upper two floors, and custom-made rounded red-orange brick, the Willey & Williams Building was ornate by Dakota standards. It prospered until the Depression as a respectable rooming house above and, variously, fruit warehouse, plumbing-supply house, and tractor-parts dealer below. Then it began to decay. By 1980 the Willey & Williams was little more than a flophouse above a flea market. Along with room after room of trash, restoration crews found the first-floor facade covered by glass and "modern" porcelain from the 1930s. Hundreds of extension cords had been plugged into a handful of sockets.

In 1984, as neighborhood buildings were beginning to undergo rehabilitation, architect Spencer Ruff of Design Development urged one of his clients, developer Don Dunham, to consider purchasing the 13,500-square-foot Willey & Williams Building. Dunham did, and Ruff convinced him to restore it. But in what style? The porcelain paneling had become historic in its own right but was too badly damaged to restore. Its installers had torn out all but one exterior cast-iron column, and, try as he might through research in local archives, Ruff could not find early drawings or a photograph to verify the building's original appearance.

An appeal in the *Sioux Falls Argus Leader* did the trick: A 1927 newspaper supplement that showed the building, and a 1914 postcard with an even better view, turned up. Ruff was thrilled. Crews soon restored glazed-brick and limestone sills, which nearly a century of South Dakota freeze-thaw cycles had ravaged. Ruined windows and sashes were replaced, but the building's long hallways and warren of rooms were retained and restored. More than $500,000 later, new tenants—including the city's minor-league basketball team—moved in.

Today, a Wallace Dow architectural drawing is a valuable keepsake, for, after he died, his heirs unceremoniously trucked his plans and blueprints to the dump. Decades later, it was only through good fortune that Dow's Willey & Williams Building did not follow suit.

*The building's rounded bricks
were custom-made. Sturdy
construction and good fortune
saved it during its flophouse and
flea market days.*

Capitol

Nashville, Tennessee

When the bumptious state of Tennessee—which had convened its legislatures in log cabins, frame homes, a school, a Presbyterian church, and a Masonic hall in four different cities—was ready for a monumental statement in its new capitol building in the early 1850s, William Strickland was an ideal choice to design it. Strickland, a protégé of Benjamin Latrobe, was an eminent Philadelphia architect and master of purist Grecian architecture who built Philadelphia's massive U.S. Mint and assisted on Latrobe's work at the U.S. Capitol.

Strickland delivered. In fact, he considered the majestic Tennessee Capitol, built on Nashville's highest knob, to be his crowning achievement. He underscored that sentiment at his death in 1854 by having himself buried, like Christopher Wren in Saint Paul's Cathedral in London, in a tomb of his design above the cornerstone. A year later, the last stone of the $1.5 million temple to democratic government, modeled after the Erectheum in Athens, was laid.

Landscaping was interrupted by the Civil War, when military governor Andrew Johnson, a Tennesseean, used the fortified "Fort Johnson" as an observation post in the 1864 Battle of Nashville. Later "renovations" did far more damage to the building than did the Yankees. During one in the 1930s, the former state Supreme Court chamber was chopped into offices. A mantelpiece was thrown away, original furniture sold, and cast-iron torchères trashed.

In the 1980s a sympathetic restoration was undertaken, beginning in the library, the shabbiest room in the building. Thirty years of direct western sunlight had rotted the draperies, and a noxious-green carpet had grown threadbare. Much of the cast-iron balcony—which had become a storeroom—was hidden behind battleship-gray plywood partitions. The restoration brought back the library's mid-19th-century appearance. In 1988 the courtroom was restored as well as possible from old photographs. Deliberately left untouched were bullet marks in a staircase bannister and a limestone column, where Governor William Gannaway Brownlow had fired at former Confederates who tried to bolt rather than vote for the Fourteenth Amendment to the Constitution, making blacks free and equal after the Civil War. The bullet holes are just one conversation piece in William Strickland's masterpiece, where, today as always, oratory—embellished by echoes resonating off its massive stone walls—is a cultivated art form.

Clark Mills's equestrian statue of Andrew Jackson outside the Tennessee Capitol was cast from the same mold as those in Jackson Square in New Orleans and Lafayette Park in Washington.
Opposite: With its cast-iron spiral staircase and stacks, this room was once the Tennessee State Library. The ironwork was ordered from Philadelphia out of a Wood & Perot catalog.

Historic Rugby

Rugby, Tennessee

Primogeniture: a fancy word that is central to the story of an American colony unlike any other. Under Great Britain's primogeniture laws in the 19th century, when a wealthy landowner died, all of his holdings passed to his eldest son—and only his eldest son. What a waste, thought reformer Thomas Hughes, England's most popular author of young people's books. Hughes and James Russell Lowell, an American poet, decided to start an American colony in which younger English sons of breeding could live industrious outdoor lives.

They found the spot for it in 1879. Both Englishmen and Americans purchased land in the "barely jackassable" prickly woods and rolling farmland above Knoxville, Tennessee. By 1884 the 450 or so inhabitants had built 70 permanent structures, including a preparatory school modeled after Hughes's alma mater, Rugby Academy in England. It gave the settlement its name.

British "younger sons" had a fine time playing lawn tennis, having tea, and discussing politics at Old Rugby. That was the problem. They were supposed to be working. (Historic Rugby Museum) Opposite: Christ Church, Episcopal, was the spiritual center of the colony. Tastes (but not much land) were cultivated elsewhere, too.

Rugby's nascent businesses included Farden's Drug Store; Cornelius Onderdonk, Builder; McKinley's Meat Market; and Lumley & Mallory General Store. At the Tabard Inn lived Rugby's resident British agriculturalist, Amos Hill, who helped the settlers plant fruit trees, berry vines, and vegetable crops. Most houses were of the Queen Anne style, with dormers, abundant gingerbread, and suitable English country estate names. In their drawing rooms could be found comforting reminders of home. In October 1887 a small Gothic sanctuary, opened for the spiritual sustenance of the colony.

But dilettantish diversions like lawn tennis and afternoon teas interrupted what little work was done. Drought parched the first decent crops, Hughes did not stay to see the colony through, and many colonists—their remittances depleting—gave up and went home.

In 1964 a schoolboy of only 16 from the nearby village of Deer Lake, Brian Stagg, visited "the town of cultured ghosts" and was enchanted by its potential. Until his untimely death in 1974 at age 26, he energized a nonprofit Rugby Restoration Association (now Historic Rugby). Well into the 1980s, using its own funds, donations, and grants in the millions of dollars—it restored eight public buildings and assisted private homeowners in their own rehabilitations. The renewal of a "failed" Utopia calls to mind the words of poet Lois Walker Johnson, who wrote of Rugby:

> *. . . if I could, I'd send word to Hughes:*
> *No dream is dead that leaves an afterglow.*

Battleship Texas

Houston, Texas

One of the rites of Texas youth is a pilgrimage to a menacing old blue-gray battleship that was not built in Texas, was never berthed there, and yet so stirs Texans' hearts that school-children from the Panhandle to the hills above Tyler hoarded quarters to save her.

Commissioned in 1912, the USS *Texas*—BB35 in Navy parlance—was once the world's most powerful dreadnought. The ship survived a U-boat attack in World War I and supported the D-Day landing at Normandy and the invasion at Okinawa in World War II, before being retired to the mothball fleet in Baltimore in preparation for an ignominious end: The government wanted to test an atomic bomb by dropping one on the redoubtable vessel. But Texans—and their congressional delegation—would have none of it. On April 21, 1948, the *Texas* was presented to the state as America's first memorial battleship, and berthed on a mud flat in the Houston shipping channel.

For 35 years it sat as a tourist attraction, disintegrating into rusted scale. About to collapse of its own weight in 1983, the ship was shifted to the state parks department, which began a desperate campaign to save it. More than $800,000 poured in from an Alcoa Aluminum recycling campaign and a statewide drive in which schoolchildren sent in sockfuls of quarters. After the legislature kicked in $7 million, and the *Texas* survived a 12-hour tug out of her mudhole to be floated to drydock in Galveston, the vessel's exterior was extensively repaired and repainted. Then "BB35 Volunteers" got to work on the interior, repainting, oiling, and rewiring in fascinating nooks such as the ship's operating room, the laundry, and the mess.

Watching the ship rain 428 shells from 14-inch guns onto German pillboxes on D-Day, Ernest Hemingway had described the USS *Texas* as "some strange and unbelievable monster." Shipshape again, the ship looms as a beloved monster in the marshes off San Jacinto Park.

There were no caps on Texas's mighty guns when it blasted away in support of the D-Day assault on Normandy, or when it propelled 2,000 rounds a day at the Japanese at Okinawa.

Shown here in 1915, three years after commissioning, the Texas was powered to a speed of 21 knots by coal-burning steam engines. The dreadnought sported the latest in radio antennae. (Texas Historical Commission)

Governor's Mansion

Austin, Texas

Not just the eyes of Texas have been upon the stately Greek Revival home of the governor of Texas. So have uncounted thousands of hands and feet, tramping and pawing through the place as if they owned it—which of course Texans do. Until Governor John Connally's wife, Idanell, pushed to get an iron fence, brick wall, and security outposts around the mansion, anyone—even a Yankee tourist—could (and often did) ring the doorbell and roust the governor's family for a chat and an impromptu peek at Sam Houston's bedroom. You could hardly blame them, since the mansion had always invited public curiosity. When it opened in 1856, Governor Elisha Pease threw such a "gay and brilliant affair" for 300 guests that it took him three days to clean up. Ninety-three years later, Governor "Pappy" Lee O'Daniel and his family gave guided tours. Organizations from all over the state routinely penciled in receptions at the governor's place, and first ladies handed out cookies and cups of tea by the thousands several times a year.

Little wonder that when self-made millionaire William P. Clements, Jr., a frequent White House guest, took office in 1979, "his expectations of a similar elegance in the Texas State house," in the words of a mansion brochure, "were hastily shattered." Clements and his wife, Rita, found cracked plaster; cigarette-burned carpeting resting on plywood that covered rotted floors; and garish red carpeting, red draperies, red flocked wallpaper, all stained by seeping rainwater. Furnishings were skimpy, owing to the tradition that governors brought their own furniture with them and took it back when they left. Among the possessions that Governor Sam Houston carted home in 1861 were 75 pounds of feathers and eight spittoons.

Governor Clements marched right across the street to the State Capitol and demanded—and got—a $1 million appropriation to restore the executive mansion, and he and his wife organized a nonprofit group called Friends of the Governor's Mansion that then raised another $3.5 million to furnish it (under the guidance of acquisitions chairman H. Ross Perot). Dallas restoration architect James L. Hendricks ordered the plaster repaired, new wallpaper applied, and wide-plank pine floors installed in most public rooms. The house was reroofed, and the porte cochere extended and given fluted Ionic columns to match those that Austin master builder Abner Cook had given the mansion in 1856. Significant new furnishings included a "Davey Crockett and the Indians" silver-plated candelabra, dated 1848; an oil portrait of the Father of Texas, Stephen F. Austin; and an Austin desk, used at his plantation on the Brazos River.

Ironically, after all their efforts on the mansion's behalf, Bill and Rita Clements, who had lived elsewhere during the restoration, were able to enjoy the grandly restored and reappointed mansion for only four months; in 1982 the governor lost his reelection bid.

The great columns of the governor's house greet one and all. The manse was almost like a gazebo in the park, the way Texas citizens once made themselves at home there, sometimes even knocking on the door and catching the governor in his nightclothes.
Opposite: Governor Elisha Pease (1853–57) kept this American Empire sofa, later given back to the mansion, at his private home in Austin. Stephen F. Austin's desk occupies another part of the library.

Ephraim Cooperative Mercantile Buildings

Ephraim, Utah

Because traditional merchants were considered profiteers, Brigham Young, head of the Church of Jesus Christ of Latter-day Saints in 1869, set up a system of retail cooperatives. At these "Zion's Cooperative Mercantile Institutions," better known by the initials ZCMI, townspeople brought the fruits of their labor for sale, trade, and redistribution.

The little alfalfa, hay, and sheep-farming town of Ephraim, snuggled in the Sanpete Valley about 75 miles south of Salt Lake City, had a ZCMI, which it called the Ephraim United Order Cooperative Mercantile. Begun in 1872 and run by Mormons whose Danish descendants had founded the town, Ephraim's Greek Revival cooperative, built of oolitic limestone, would also become the home of the Sanpete Stake Academy in 1888, a tiny church, secondary school, and college. A short distance south was a limestone-block granary, run by the Women's Relief Society.

By the turn of the century, the ZCMI building became a farm-implement store, then later an automobile shop, and finally a roller mill—where grain was fashioned into huge rolls for livestock. After a one-story structure was built connecting it with the granary, their functions were switched—the granary becoming a mill and the former co-op and schoolhouse turning into a storehouse for grain. As a result, both structures were altered and damaged.

In the 1950s the mill closed, and the Bank of Ephraim became the reluctant owner of two outdated and abandoned buildings. The city ordered demolition, felling first the one-story connector. But the two older buildings were rescued after 70 Ephraim citizens took over the $700 monthly mortgage payments. In the 1970s, a short-lived plan to turn the co-op building into a community theater got far enough that grants were obtained to fix its deteriorating roof and restore its kingpost trusses. But the theater scheme collapsed when its principal backer moved, and the old co-op and granary remained empty eyesores through most of the 1980s.

Then council member Bob Stoddard spearheaded a complex fund-raising effort, which included state loans, raising $650,000 to assist in restoring both buildings. First came the co-op. "There were cracks that you could put your hand through," says Allen Roberts, a Salt Lake City preservation architect who worked on the project. "They had bricked in all the original openings so the grain wouldn't fall out." The co-op became a crafts store—a cooperative just like the old ZCMI. Then crews restored the granary as an art gallery, duplicating its old, missing, octagonal cupola to help bring light into the upper floor.

"The beauty of the restored buildings amazed people," says Ephraim mayor Robert E. Harnick. "Now I think we would be run out of town if we even mentioned tearing them down."

*Profits from the mercantile
association were plowed back
into support for local crafts and
factories. The beehive symbol,
ubiquitous throughout Utah,
symbolized industriousness.*

Officers' Row

Colchester and Essex, Vermont

Rank had its privileges at Fort Ethan Allen, the U.S. Cavalry fort built between 1894 and 1904 near Lake Champlain and named for Vermont's Revolutionary War hero. Commissioned officers lived in 22 stately Colonial Revival red-brick homes on Officers' Row along Dalton Drive, fronting the parade ground. The Drury brick, Vermont slate, granite, and marble buildings were standard army, and solid, right out of the Quartermaster General's plans.

The last of the military's horses at Fort Ethan Allen was sold in 1934, and the stalls converted to automotive use. When the fort closed in 1960, its buildings and 787 of its 1,000 acres devolved to the Vermont National Guard—then to the University of Vermont and Saint Michael's College for use as student housing. In the early 1980s, having been subjected to the indignities that undergraduates are known to deliver, the dilapidated units were abandoned entirely and, in 1987, offered for sale. In 1990 the Vermont Housing Finance Agency purchased Officers' Row for $1.5 million and retained Preservation Investments of Middlebury, Vermont, to assist in restoring the site. That it did, following the Secretary of the Interior's Standards for Rehabilitation. In order to keep the units affordable, much was left to the new owners, who were given handbooks with instructions on how to restore woodwork, cabinets, and fir floors. Seventy-seven units opened for sale in 1992 at bargain prices. Loft apartments, at $62,000, were snapped up first, and a new, moderate-income community was created.

Gone from the parade grounds is the proud Third U.S. Cavalry on snorting horses. But Officers' Row has sprung to life again, and Fort Ethan Allen's stables, a blacksmith shop, several cavalry barracks, and other remnants of those gallant times await their own revival.

Once abandoned and bedraggled, the stately Officers' Row buildings were rehabilitated into affordable condominiums. Loft apartments overlooking the parade grounds were snapped up first.

Officers' Row at Fort Ethan Allen was a perfect place for a quiet wagon ride, c. 1910. There were plenty of rigs and mounts to choose from at this cavalry post. (Special Collections, University of Vermont Library)

William Seward Webb and his male friends would often retire to the Game Room for brandy, cigars, billiards, and the stories behind Dr. Webb's hunting trophies over the fireplace.

The Tea Room, shown in both historic and modern views, was used for breakfast and informal dinners. Now diners peruse the menu and sip aperitifs here before dinner at Shelburne House. After the house was essentially abandoned, chunks of plaster fell from the ceilings throughout the residence, requiring major restoration work. (T. E. Marr, Shelburne Farms Collection)

Bolling Haxall House

Richmond, Virginia

Richmond, Va.,
May, 1894

We, the undersigned, propose to organize a Woman's Club, the aim and purpose of which shall be to cultivate Music, Dramatic Performances and Literature. In addition—for the pleasure and instruction of the members—two entertainments will be given each month, and at the discretion of the Club distinguished lecturers will be secured.

Thus began an invitation from 14 energetic Richmond women to 54 other women. Lunsford Lomax Lewis, spouse of the club's organizer, was heard to react, "What is to become of us poor husbands? I never find all the buttons on my clothes, nor are my socks without holes, since Jane started her club." The Woman's Club of Richmond met in rented rooms until 1900, when, for $20,000, the members purchased an 1858 Italianate, stucco-over-brick villa once belonging to Bolling Walker Haxall, president of the Old Dominion Iron and Nail Works.

Fortunate to have escaped Richmond's flames at the close of the Civil War, the already exquisite home was further embellished by its second owner, physician Francis T. Willis, who bought it for $28,000 in 1869 and gave it its stunning walnut double-spiral staircase. The Woman's Club purchased the house from Willis's grandson after resourceful members, denied a mortgage loan in their hometown, hopped a train to Baltimore to get one.

Today, their clubhouse features semicircular balconies, double-arched cast-iron lintels, a square cupola, and an extraordinary pendant over the central third-story window. Inside, walnut window and door frames are elaborately carved with cartouches—scroll-like ornaments—in the center of each arch. Tromp l'oeil effects in the library were recaptured as part of a multistage restoration begun in 1986 and partially underwritten by the Historic Richmond Foundation. Workers also replaced ponderous venetian blinds with restored pocket window shutters and lace curtains and returned historic gasoliers to their original appearance.

Once described by a club member as "exciting as a load o' hay," the formerly bland, uniform-green 1916 auditorium turned neo-Grec. Interior designer C. Dudley Brown and architect Richard S. Slater added Pompeiian red-marble wainscoting, elaborate friezes, and a wall covering featuring medallions with the classical elements of Earth, Water, Fire, and Wind around the clerestory windows. On the outside, restorers replaced rotted woodwork and replicated the original dark brown with a red-and-brown-trim paint scheme.

The club that once had to rent rooms and, during the Depression, could not afford $50 to repair a damaged balustrade above the front portico, had come quite a distance.

This beautiful walnut spiral staircase held tragic memories for the house's second owner whose 16-year-old granddaughter died after a headlong fall down the stairs.

Wells Theatre

Norfolk, Virginia

There was a time when theater chains operated throughout the United States. Not movie houses: legitimate theaters. One, the 40-theater Wells Brothers group, stretched from Evansville, Indiana, to Jacksonville, Florida. Its flagship was in Norfolk in Tidewater Virginia.

The 1,650-seat Wells opened on August 26, 1913, with a production of *The Merry Countess,* and that year alone, performances included *Ben-Hur* (with a cast of 200 and horses), an epic play on the Jews of Siberia, and a session with Pauline the Hypnotist. In a preview of technology to come, there was also a silent movie about the Boy Scouts of America.

By World War II, when Norfolk was crammed with sailors, the theater—which a later Wells publication called "an inchoate version of a Renaissance palazzo"—had switched primarily to burlesque. "B" movies followed the war, and then, in the 1960s and early 1970s, came X-rated flicks. A cinderblock wall was erected behind the movie screen so the Jamaican Room, a go-go lounge that the theater's own written history describes as "one of Norfolk's sleaziest gin mills," could fill the stage. By the mid-1970s the Wells was abandoned and taken over by the city of Norfolk, and in 1979, after hasty and superficial repairs, in which the theater was hosed down, painted, and given a rudimentary light and sound system, the Virginia Stage Company—southeastern Virginia's only professional, nonprofit theater company—opened its inaugural season there.

In March 1986 a glorious restoration began, financed through a $3.85 million campaign heavily underwritten by Central Fidelity Bank, the Norfolk Southern Corporation, and the city. The Wells's intricate marquee, pantile roof, stained glass in the lobby rotunda, and robed Grecian caryatids "holding up" the balcony were all refurbished. So, too, was the great ceiling mural above the stage—a copy of Sir Lawrence Alma-Tadema's sensual "A Reading from Homer," completed in 1885. Project restoration architect John Paul Hanbury says he took particular delight in the restoration of a series of plaster faces that ring the auditorium. "You could sit through a boring play, if there ever was one," he says, "and count the number of faces—and the flagons around the stage and the rosettes and murals, and, up on the ceiling, the cabbage roses. There's no way today you could find the craftsmen to execute all of those delightful excesses."

A fanciful facade attracted customers during the Wells Theatre's heyday in the early years of the 20th century, and continues to attract theatergoers now.

Restoration architect John Paul Hanbury says he took particular delight in bringing back the plaster faces that ring the Wells's lush "Theater Edwardian" auditorium.

Patsy Clark's Restaurant

Spokane, Washington

One of the men who made millions as a partner in the legendary Anaconda copper mine near Butte, Montana, was a former gold and silver miner named Patrick "Patsy" Clark. By 1895 he had moved to Spokane and was ready to build his family a palatial home. He engaged Spokane's Kirtland K. Cutter, a European-trained architect and world traveler. Clark issued Cutter virtually an unlimited budget, and, as the saying goes, Cutter exceeded it. An estimated $1 million went into the Clark mansion and furnishings.

Armed with Clark's "nothing but the best" blank check, Cutter was off to Italy, where he chose the mansion's sepia sandstone trim and "gopher wood" dining room paneling, into which 29 different visages of monks' heads would be carved; to Turkey for rugs, one of which cost $17,000; to Saint Louis to pick the exterior brick; to London for a grandfather clockworks with Whittington and Westminster chimes; and to New York for the clock's case, which has gold-plated filigree around a silver-plated dial with blue-steel serpentine hands. These were only a few of the fabulous materials and furnishings shipped by rail to Clark in frontier Spokane.

Patsy Clark drowned under mysterious circumstances in 1915, at which time $1 million of his holdings could not be accounted for. From 1926, when his wife, Mary, moved to one of the property's carriage house apartments, to 1977, the Clark Mansion was another family's home, a girls' boarding house, an unsuccessful restaurant, and the Francis-Lester Inn and reception facility.

In 1977 Seattle restaurateurs Chuck Quinn and Ken Bauer, and their friend Tony Anderson, a professor of urban development at Eastern Washington University in Cheney, bought the house—including all its extravagant furnishings—for $210,000. It took them six years to convince neighbors and the city zoning board to agree to let them reopen the mansion as a fine restaurant. In preparation, they remade several bedrooms and a bride's changing room into private-function rooms, carefully added a glass enclosure around a side porch to create a solarium, and moved other furniture to create opulent private dining spaces.

Principal owner Quinn says he dreamed of running a restaurant in the lavish Francis-Lester Inn in Spokane. "Tony Anderson called about buying the Patsy Clark mansion," he says, "but I didn't know till I went to look at it that it and the Francis-Lester were one in the same."

Patsy Clark made a fortune in the mines of Montana and Idaho—and spent a fortune on the grandest house in Spokane. His architect, Kirtland K. Cutter, exceeded an unlimited budget in completing it. Opposite: Many of the Clark Mansion's 26 rooms, with their Roman, Moorish, Chinese, and Egyptian architecture and fabulous furnishings, are stunning, but the smaller spaces are also delightful for dinner.

Arthurdale Planned Community

Arthurdale, West Virginia

Into West Virginia's Scotts Run coal district along the Monongahela River in 1933, in the depths of the Depression, rode First Lady Eleanor Roosevelt. Scotts Run had become a cauldron of anarchy and despair after union miners struck when their 22-cents-a-ton wages were cut and they were evicted from company shacks. The First Lady left appalled, hurried home, and demanded that something be done. Within weeks, an unprecedented mobilization was moving destitute families to farms and subsistence homesteads in 99 planned communities in several states. Arthurdale, a dozen or so miles from Scotts Run, was the first of them all.

Agents surreptitiously bought a 1,018-acre farm for $35,000 from Richard Arthur, who was raising fighting cocks and livestock. Soon men were clearing land and raising prefabricated houses in the new Arthurdale Planned Community. At Mrs. Roosevelt's insistence—and to the envy of neighbors—electricity and plumbing were provided to every Arthurdale house. The Civil Works Administration paid women to make curtains, sheets, and pillowcases for each house, and the community's Mountaineer Craftsmen's Cooperative crafted hand-made furniture.

Eleanor Roosevelt makes one of her frequent, often unannounced, visits to Arthurdale in the mid-1930s. (Howard B. Allen, West Virginia and Regional History Collection, West Virginia University Library)

Andrew Wolfe was one of the original homesteaders. He began as a laborer and worked his way up to manager of the town store. "People in Preston County, a few of 'em, turned up their noses at us," he says. "They thought we was takin' handouts, something for nothing. It wasn't so. All they gave me was a home that I was paying for, and a chance to make a living."

Almost all of Arthurdale's original homes still stand; most were carefully landscaped and modernized over the years. But communal functions dissolved with the government's departure by 1947, and the liquidated community buildings deteriorated badly. The picture brightened as the community coalesced around resident Glenna Williams's plans for a 50th reunion of original homesteaders in 1984. A foundation, Arthurdale Heritage, was organized; and members raised more than $108,000 to begin restoring common structures. At the old administration building, for instance, volunteers repaired the roof, fixed the plumbing, replaced damaged wallboard with a similar Celotex material, and cleaned the exterior stone walls. "It helped us develop a new sense of pride in who we were," Williams says. "This is an ongoing restoration not just of buildings, but of a spirit of community. Young people as well as old are part of it."

*Arthurdale's old administration
building—now its museum
and information center—was
full of political posters, piles
of furniture bought at
auctions, and barn swallows
before restoration.*

Parade Wagons at Circus World Museum

Baraboo, Wisconsin

I t was not a ringmaster's whistle that heralded "Circus Day" in every decent-sized burg in America for the 20 years on each side of the turn of the century. It was the synchronized clopping of draft horses, mingled with the rousing tunes of a brass band atop a four-ton wagon at the head of the grand street parade bearing the circus from the train depot into town.

Behind the bandwagon rolled up to 25 chariots; tableau wagons; mounted cages carrying big cats and other exotic animals; baggage wagons disguised as theme floats; and, raucously bringing up the rear, a steam calliope, which became the very symbol of the circus. All were painted gaudy colors, especially silver and gold, the better to impress paying customers.

Cousins to rugged brewery wagons and omnibuses, circus wagons were built by many of the same wheelwrights who brought in master carvers to create the wagons' intricate wood theme panels. Circus wagons had to be sturdy, with massive wheels and powerful springs and a cumbersome braking wheel, because they pulled every pole and rope, every lion, every sideshow booth and hire-wire net and popcorn stand—and every person—in the company.

As the number of train-borne circuses dwindled from a dozen in 1920 to a handful by 1940, two in 1956, and one today, these glittering mastodons were shunted into obscurity. One by one, circus wagons found their way into carnivals, collectors' garages, or circus storage sheds. Hundreds rotted and rusted in open fields.

But in 1959 a man who owned just one of these magical wagons brightened their bleak future. John M. Kelley, a former attorney for the Ringling Brothers Circus, opened "Circus World" as a museum in Baraboo, where the five Ringlings had founded their show. Now owned by the Wisconsin State Historical Society and run without state support by the Historic Sites Foundation, Circus World has grown into a 60-acre site housing more than 200 vehicles, 60 vintage railroad cars, and its own big top from the days the Ringling circus wintered there.

Many donated or purchased circus wagons arrive terribly decayed, their paint blistered or faded, undercarriages broken or modified, and carvings cracked or missing. In its own shop, Circus World restores them all. "We first determine what's original," says Fred Dahlinger, Jr., director of Circus World's Parkinson Library, "then bring it back, using original colors, restoring the carvings or creating accurate wood-carved replacements." The elaborate wagons spend most of their days indoors. But on some summer days, they are hauled out and displayed along the Baraboo River. And one weekend each July, they again take a train ride to Milwaukee, 90 miles away, where they rumble one more time in the Great Circus Parade.

The "America" wagon was part of a 1903 series of four theme wagons ("Africa," "Asia," and "Europe" were the others). In 1940 it was converted into a calliope wagon, its form today.

The "Golden Age of Chivalry"
wagon, built in 1903, carried a
"damsel in distress" and men in
medieval costume who
(repeatedly) slew the dragon
that was tormenting her.

Top: Gordon Lillie included his portrait as "Pawnee Bill" on this 1903 wagon from his Wild West show. One of the founders of the American Bison Society, Lillie helped save the buffalo from extinction.

Above: This lion-and-snake tableau wagon was built for a trained wild animal show in Germany. Later, in the Ringling Brothers, Barnum & Bailey Circus, it was a luggage wagon. Overleaf: This elephant wagon paraded for only five years in the 1920s. Its carvings were then removed to decorate a circus headquarters and a theme park.

Aladdin Tipple

Aladdin, Wyoming

Scruffy, intrepid gold and silver miners in the Gabby Hayes mold are a part of the colorful lore of the Old West. Ignored are the miners who extracted the coal that fueled the smelters and the railroads that got the hard-rock ore to market. Nowhere in a Zane Grey novel is there an account of a prospector scrabbling down a hillside shouting, "Coal! I've stuck coal!"

One coal mine was first dug in 1898 near the minuscule northeast Wyoming settlement of Aladdin. Mules pulled its coal in cars along rails to the mine entrance, where a giant tipple—a spindly structure of crude timbers and milled lumber—carried it in chutes down the steep hillside to railroad cars below. The chutes self-sorted the fuel into lump- or egg-sized pieces. Later the tipple's "hoist house," clad in sheet metal salvaged from cyanide canisters, held a motor that replaced the mules, hauling the coal cars along a cable from the depths of the mine.

Production at Aladdin reached 40,000 tons in 1901 but was down to 1,000 tons by 1911, and the mine would close a decade or so later. Until 1946, when the mine entrance was blown shut, local families continued to dig some coal for use in heating and cooking. The tipple gradually began to slump and tilt, but despite the best efforts of nature and vandals, it stood.

In the late 1980s some of Aladdin's 15 or so adult residents took a fresh look at their creaking, weathered tipple. Ruby Hutchinson, who, along with her husband, Albert, owned a large ranch outside Aladdin, brought together residents, county commissioners, and preservationists to discuss restoring the historic structure. Norma Hendricks, Albert Hutchinson's sister, who had inherited the tipple site, agreed to donate it and the mineral rights to the Crook County commissioners once restoration was completed. The residents retained two Montana firms to prepare a feasibility study and complete the $300,000 restoration. Funds came from the federal Abandoned Mine Lands program, in which coal operators pay from 15 to 35 cents a ton from their production for the environmental sins of their predecessors. Crews righted and braced the tipple, then added fencing and interpretive signage. They also cordoned off a patch of ground under the tipple for a "bioremediation" study, suggested by a Black Hills State University professor and student. Scientists analyze the grayish, acidic coal slack, in which a fungus, *Pisolithus tinctorius*, thrives—transferring nutrients to the roots of nearby plants.

At the restored tipple's 1992 dedication, Gary Beach, program manager at the Wyoming Department of Environmental Quality, noted mining's role in Wyoming's heritage, adding, "I hope the restored Aladdin Tipple will stand as a symbol of the hard work and tough conditions that many of our ancestors endured to develop and extract the state's mineral wealth."

If you think the Aladdin Tipple looks rickety now, you should have seen it in the 1980s, when residents were betting how long it would take for the leaning structure to tumble. It's now well reinforced and braced.

Lake Hotel

Yellowstone National Park, Wyoming

Until artist Thomas Moran and photographer William H. Jackson so captivated the nation with their stunning depictions of gorges and effervescing geysers on Montana Territory's Yellowstone River, only fur traders, survey expeditions, poachers, Indian tribes, and health fanatics in search of thermal waters had paid the area much mind. The only accommodations were 12-square-foot rooms at McCartney's, a strictly bring-your-own-blanket hotel. Public enthusiasm for the area eventually led to Congress's setting aside two million acres as Yellowstone National Park in 1872.

The Northern Pacific Railroad cornered the market on travel to the park via its depot in Livingston, Montana [see p. 180], and it ran stagecoaches that jostled visitors over the dirt "Grand Loop." The railroad also backed the company that won the right to build hotels along the loop. The first, on a bluff overlooking Yellowstone Lake, largest lake in North America above 7,000 feet, resembled railroad right-of-way hotels. Barrackslike, made of clapboard painted yellow, with a veranda and "widow's walk" observation deck, the Lake Hotel opened in 1891.

By 1905 the Northern Pacific had sold its interests in the Lake Hotel to a Montana banker, Harry Child, who embarked on an ambitious expansion project. His architect was Robert Charles Reamer, who gave the Lake a grand, neoclassical look with a new wing of guest rooms, four 50-foot Ionic columns, a solarium, and a series of false balconies. Almost overnight, the Lake had become a comfortably rustic resort hotel.

Over the next seven decades the Lake had more downs than ups—closing three times and undergoing remodelings that left it with birch-veneer and canteen-metal furnishings. Alarmed by complaints about shoddy conditions, the National Park Service in 1979 purchased the concessionaire's assets and granted a long-term lease to TW Services, a company that ran properties in a number of national parks. Over the next few years during bitterly cold winter months when the park was closed, TW Services undertook a wholesale restoration of the old Lake Hotel, including the installation of a new foundation more than three football fields in length. Vintage-1920 Lake Hotel doors, sconces, wicker chairs, writing tables, and plant stands were located in warehouses and the demolished Canyon Hotel, reconditioned, and put back in service.

Yellowstone's terrible fire of 1988, which destroyed millions of acres of forest, luckily raged far from the Lake Hotel. Just as torched areas were left to regenerate, the grounds around the Lake Hotel have not been landscaped. Flowers are wild, bison roam among the pines, and a natural landmark of more than 80 years' standing can still be seen: It's a series of ruts in the soil that have survived from the days when visitors arrived on a jouncing Concord stagecoach.

*In a park full of rustic log
structures, Robert Charles
Reamer's neoclassical Lake
Hotel was a surprising picture
of refinement, with a solarium,
porte cochere, and commodious
guest rooms.*

Suggested Reading List

This listing represents the authors' selection of helpful printed resources about many of the sites featured in *America Restored.*

AFRICAN MEETING HOUSE

Hayden, Robert C. *The African Meeting House in Boston.* Boston: Museum of Afro American History, 1987.

BILTMORE HOUSE

Biltmore Estate: House, Gardens, Winery. Asheville, N.C.: The Biltmore Co., 1991.

CARROLL HOUSE

Ulmer, Avelon and Kelsh, Ramona, eds. *Fullerton 1887–1987: A Century of Community.* Fullerton, N.D.: Fullerton Centennial Committee, 1986.

CHICAGO THEATER

Chicago Theatre: A Sixtieth Anniversary Salute. Chicago: Theatre Historical Society annual, 1981.

CITIZENS NATIONAL BANK & TRUST CO.

Morgan, H. Wayne and Morgan, Anne Hodges. *Oklahoma: A Bicentennial History.* New York: W. W. Norton & Company, Inc., 1977.

CLEVEHOLM CASTLE

Kenny, Norma. *The Hidden Place: Redstone.* Redstone, Colo.: Redstone Press, 1992.

COBBLESTONE FARM

Preservation for Cobblestone Farm. Ann Arbor, Mich.: Report of the Cobblestone Farm Historic District Study Committee, 1982.

COLORADO CHAUTAUQUA

Galey, Mary. *The Grand Assembly: The Story of Life at the Colorado Chautauqua.* Boulder, Colo.: First Flatiron Press, 1981.

COVERED BRIDGES OF RUSH COUNTY

Weber, Wayne M. *Covered Bridges in Indiana.* Midland, Mich.: Norwood Institute, 1977.

CUSTER COUNTY ART CENTER

McDaniel, Susan R. and Sanford, Dena L. *Beautiful City of Miles.* Miles City, Mont.: Custer County Society for the Preservation of Local Folklore, Legend, History, and Tradition, 1991.

DEADWOOD HISTORIC DISTRICT

Milton, John. *South Dakota: A Bicentennial History.* New York: W.W. Norton & Co., 1977.

Parker, Watson. *Deadwood: The Golden Years.* Lincoln, Neb.: University of Nebraska Press, 1981.

EMLEN PHYSICK HOUSE

Pratt, Anne Biddle. *The Emlen Physick House Museum: A Victorian House Tour.*
Fletcher, Ohio: Cam-Tech Publishing, 1990.

FLAGLER COLLEGE

Graham, Thomas. *Flagler's Magnificent Hotel Ponce de Leon* and *Flagler's Grand Hotel
Alcazar* (monographs). Saint Augustine, Fla.: Saint Augustine Historical Society,
1989.

FORDYCE BATHHOUSE

Beddinger, M. S. *Valley of the Vapors: Hot Springs National Park.* Philadelphia:
Eastern National Park & Monument Association, 1991.

Brown, Dee. *The American Spa: Hot Springs, Arkansas.* Little Rock: Rose Publishing
Company, 1982.

FOURTH WARD SCHOOL

McDonald, Douglas. *Virginia City and the Silver Region of the Comstock Lode.*
Las Vegas: Nevada Publications, 1982.

FRONTIER NURSING SERVICE

Breckinridge, Mary. *Wide Neighborhoods: A Story of the Frontier Nursing Service.*
Lexington, Ky.: The University Press of Kentucky, 1981.

GELDNER SAWMILL

Zimmerman, John T. *The Geldner Sawmill.* (manuscript) Elysian, Minn.: Le Sueur
County Historical Society, 1985.

GRAND CANYON RAILWAY

Richmond, Al. *Cowboys, Miners, Presidents & Kings: The Story of the Grand Canyon
Railway.* Williams, Ariz.: Grand Canyon Railway, 1989.

GRINNAN VILLA

Howard, Hugh. *The Preservationist's Progress: Architectural Adventures in Conserving
Yesterday's Houses.* New York: Farrar, Strauss & Giroux, 1991.

Starr, S. Frederick. *Southern Comfort: The Garden District of New Orleans,
1800–1900.* Cambridge: Massachusetts Institute of Technology, 1989.

HISTORIC RUGBY

Dickinson, W. Calvin. *Morgan County.* Tennessee County History Series. Memphis,
Tenn.: Memphis State University Press, 1987.

Wichmann, Patricia Guion. *Rugby: A Great Man's Dream.* Self-published 1963
monograph available from Historic Rugby, Inc., Rugby, Tenn.

INDEPENDENCE HALL

Marshall, Paul D. *Historic Structure Report: West Virginia Independence Hall/
Wheeling Custom House.* Charleston, W.Va.: Paul D. Marshall & Associates, 1986.

KIRKWOOD RANCH

Jordan, Grace. *Home Below Hell's Canyon.* New York: Thomas Y. Crowell Co., 1954.

LAKE HOTEL

Dittl, Barbara and Mallmann, Joanne. *Plain to Fancy: The Story of the Lake Hotel.* Boulder, Colo.: Roberts Rinehart, Inc., 1987.

LONGWOOD

Gleason, David King. *The Great Houses of Natchez.* Jackson, Miss.: University Press of Mississippi, 1986.

Lane, Mills. *Architecture of the Old South: Mississippi & Alabama.* New York: Abbeville Press, 1989.

MAIN BUILDING AT ELLIS ISLAND

Novotny, Ann. *Strangers at the Door. Ellis Island, Castle Garden, and the Great Migration to America.* New York: Chatham Press, 1972.

MILES BREWTON HOUSE

Lane, Mills. *Architecture of the Old South: South Carolina.* Savannah, Ga.: Beehive Press, 1984.

MILWAUKEE GRAIN EXCHANGE ROOM

Zimmerman, H. Russell. *Magnificent Milwaukee: Architectural Treasures, 1850–1920.* Milwaukee: Milwaukee Public Museum, 1987.

PARADE WAGONS AT CIRCUS WORLD MUSEUM

Goldsmith, Lynn. *Circus Dreams.* New York: Rizzoli International Publications, Inc., 1991.

PENDLETON DEPOT

Macnab, Gordon. *A Century of News and People in the East Oregonian.* Pendleton, Ore.: East Oregonian Publishing, 1975.

ROCKWOOD

Sullivan, Patricia. *Romantic Rockwood: Rural Gothic Villa in Delaware.* Wilmington, Del.: Rockwood Museum, 1982.

ROSENBAUM HOUSE

Rosenbaum, Alvin. *Usonia: Frank Lloyd Wright's Design for America.* Washington, D.C.: The Preservation Press, 1993.

Sergeant, John. *Frank Lloyd Wright's Usonian Houses: The Case for Organic Architecture.* New York: Watson-Guptill Publications, 1975.

RUSSIAN BISHOP'S HOUSE

U.S. Department of the Interior, National Park Service, Denver Service Center, *The Russian Bishop's House: Historic Structure Report,* prepared by James D. Mote, n.d.

The Russian Bishop's House: Legacy of an Empire, 1842. (pamphlet) Anchorage,
Alaska: Alaska Natural History Association, 1992.

SAINT JAMES HOTEL

Marvin, Patrice Avon and Vrooman, Nicholas Curchin. *If Walls Could Talk: A Story
of the Old St. James.* Red Wing, Minn.: Red Wing Hotel Corporation, 1984.

SAINT PETER'S EPISCOPAL CHURCH

Lindsley, J. Elliott. *A History of Saint Peter's Church.* Morristown, N.J.: Rector,
Wardens, and Vestrymen of Saint Peter's Church, 1952.

SAINT PHILOMENA CHURCH

Daws, Gavan. *Holy Man: Father Damien of Molokai.* Honolulu: University of Hawaii
Press, 1973.

Law, Anwei Skinsnes (with photographs by Wayne Levin). *Kalaupapa: A Portrait.*
Honolulu, Hawaii: Arizona Memorial Museum Association and Bishop Museum
Press, 1989.

SALT LAKE CITY AND COUNTY BUILDING

Higgins, Raymond Elmer. "The Architectural History of the Salt Lake City and
County Building." Master's thesis, University of Utah Department of Art, 1978.

SAN JOSÈ DE GRACIA CHURCH

Kessel, John L. *The Missions of New Mexico Since 1776.* Albuquerque: University of
New Mexico Press, 1980.

SHAKERTOWN

Morse, Flo. *The Story of the Shakers.* Woodstock, Vt.: Countryman Press, 1986.

SHAY HEXAGON HOUSE

Koch, Michael. *Titan of the Timber.* New York: World Press, Inc., 1971

SHELBURNE FARMS

Sherman, Joe. *The House at Shelburne Farms.* Middlebury, Vt.: Paul S. Eriksson, 1986.

STRAWBERY BANKE

Strawbery Banke Official Guidebook. Portsmouth, N.H.: Strawbery Banke, Inc., 1982

TENNESSEE CAPITOL

Daniel, Jean Houston and Daniel, Price. *Executive Mansions and Capitols of America.*
Waukesha, Wis.: Country Beautiful, 1969.

Gadski, Mary Ellen. "The Tennessee State Capitol: An Architectural History."
Tennessee Historical Quarterly 47 (Summer 1988).

McBride, Robert M., ed. *More Landmarks of Tennessee History.* Nashville: Tennessee
Historical Society, 1969.